Cantos de adolescencia
Songs of Youth

Recovering the U.S. Hispanic Literary Heritage
Board of Editorial Advisors

Cantos de adolescencia
Songs of Youth
(1932-1937)

by
Américo Paredes

Translated with an Introduction and Annotations by
B.V. Olguín
&
Omar Vásquez Barbosa

Arte Público Press
Houston, Texas

This volume is made possible through grants from the Brown Foundation, the City of Houston through the Houston Arts Alliance, the Exemplar Program, a program of Americans for the Arts in collaboration with the LarsonAllen Public Services Group, funded by the Ford Foundation, and the M.D. Anderson Foundation.

Recovering the past, creating the future

Arte Público Press
University of Houston
452 Cullen Performance Hall
Houston, Texas 77204-2004

Cover design by ExacType
All photos courtesy of the Nettie Lee Benson Latin American collection, University of Texas Libraries, The University of Texas at Austin.

Paredes, Américo
Cantos de adolescencia = Songs of Youth: 1932-1937 / by Américo Paredes; translated with introduction and annotation by B.V. Olguín & Omar Vásquez Barbosa.
p. cm. — (Recovering the U.S. Hispanic Literary Heritage Project publication)
ISBN: 978-155885-495-6 (alk. paper)
1. Paredes, Américo—Translations into English. I. Olguín, B.V., 1965- II. Vásquez Barbosa, Omar. III. Title. IV. Title: Songs of Youth.
PQ7297.A1A2 2007
860—dc22

2007060687
CIP

∞ The paper used in this publication meets the requirements of the American National Standard for Information Sciences—Permanence of Paper for Printed Library Materials, ANSI Z39.48-1984.

7 8 9 0 1 2 3 4 5 6 10 9 8 7 6 5 4 3 2 1

Para don Américo
con todo respeto

y para las poetas chicanas y los poetas chicanos
que se han inspirado en su vida y obra

Contents

Américo Paredes
Literary Chronology

1915 Born September 3, in Brownsville, Texas.

1932 Wins High School poetry contest representing Brownsville High School.

1934 Wins statewide poetry contest sponsored by Trinity University while a student at Brownsville High School. Paredes' sonnet submission, "Night," is published in the *Valley Morning Star*, May 3.

1930s Reads and writes poetry in collaboration with advertising campaigns by local Mexican-American merchants in Brownsville.

1935 Wins academic contest for essay on Miguel Cervantes de Saavedra while a student at Brownsville Junior College.

1935 Writes first version of landmark poem, "The Mexico-Texan" and publishes it in the *Brownsville Herald* a year later.

1935-40s Active literary exchanges with writers from the Lower Rio Grande Writers Circle. Members send unpublished poems and *décimas* in correspondence and hold regular meetings to discuss literature and political philosophy.

1936 Publishes poem "Guadalupe la Chinaca" in unidentified local newspaper (probably the *Brownsville Herald*) on June 7.

Sketches plan for first poetry collection to be called *Black Roses*. Some of the poems subsequently included in *Cantos de adolescencia*. Others remain lost or were destroyed by the author.

1936-40s Wrote journalism features on folklore for the *Brownsville Herald*.

Writes first novel *George Washington Gómez*.

1937 Publishes *Cantos de adolescencia* with Librería Española, San Antonio, Texas. Prominent businessmen and writers honor Paredes, who had come to be known as "El joven bardo," at literary banquet in Matamoros, Mexico.

La Prensa (San Antonio) publishes a two-page special pull-out section of excerpts from *Cantos de adolescencia*, October 18.

Gregorio Garza Flores, editor of *El Regional* (Matamoros, Mexico), encourages Paredes to write prose fiction through correspondence dated August 25.

Noted University of Texas librarian Carlos E. Castañeda praises *Cantos de adolescencia* and predicts Paredes "will obtain the success he deserves and will vindicate the reputation of his people" (*obtendrá el éxito que merece y vindicará el nombre de su raza*) in a letter dated October 25.

Receives award of decorative leather jacket for *Cantos de adolescencia* from *The Arizona Quarterly*.

1938 Publishes poem "Mi pueblo de amanecer," dedicated to fellow writer Sabas Klahn, in unknown Brownsville newspaper (probably the *Brownsville Herald*) in May.

First documented payment for unknown poem published in *Texas Farming and Citriculture* trade magazine.

1939 Writes "The Hammon and the Beans," which is published in the *Texas Observer* on April 18, 1963.

1940-50s Wrote column for *El Universal* (Mexico City).

1941 Publishes Spanish version of "The Mexico-Texan" ("*El Mexico-Texano*") in *La Voz* (Brownsville), August 31.

University of Texas Library requests a copy of *Cantos de adolescencia* for its archives.

1944 Wrote Prologue to fellow Rio Grande Writers Circle poet Manuel Cruz' collection of poetry, *Romanso Azul*. An early draft of Paredes' prologue is included in the Américo Paredes Papers, but Cruz' manuscript remains lost.

1944-46 Drafted into the U.S. Army in 1944. Wrote as enlisted soldier for U.S. Army newspaper *Stars and Stripes*, and served as a political editor who covered the war crimes trials of Japanese officers.

1945 Featured poetry performance with musicians in Brownsville, Texas, November 21-22.

1946-50 Works as uniformed member of the American Red Cross stationed in various countries throughout Asia. Imbeds unpublished poems in letters home to his wife on American Red Cross stationary, and also lays out sketches for borderlands stories and novellas on U.S. government stationary.

1948 Writes the short story "Over the Waves" published in the *New Mexico Review* in 1953.

1951 Graduates with B.A. in English from the University of Texas at Austin.

1953 Receives M.A. in English from the University of Texas at Austin.

1955 While still a graduate student at the University of Texas at Austin, wins prizes for a novel, *The Shadow* and unidentified short story.

1956 Receives Ph.D. from the University of Texas at Austin at age 40.

1958 Dissertation, *With His Pistol in His Hand: A Border Ballad and its Hero*, is published by the University of Texas Press. Paredes receives death threats for his critical treatment of the Texas Rangers.

1963 Short story "The Hammon and the Beans" is published in the *Texas Observer* on April 18.

1966 With Joseph Castle and M.M., Cole Press publishes *Folk Music of Mexico: Book for the Guitar No. 671*, Chicago, Illinois.

1968 Publishes scholarly folio *The Décima on the Texas-Mexican Border*.

1976 Publishes *A Texas-Mexican Cancionero: Folksongs of the Lower Border*, University of Illinois Press.

1989 Awarded the Charles Frankel Prize from the National Endowment for the Humanities.

1990 Publishes *George Washington Gómez: A Mexico-texan Novel*, Arte Público Press.

1991 Publishes collection of poetry, *Between Two Worlds*, Arte Público Press. Paredes claims in introduction to have destroyed many early poems.

Awarded *El Águila Azteca*, the Order of the Aztec Eagle, the highest honor bestowed on foreign nationals by the government of Mexico.

1993 Publishes *Uncle Remus con Chile,* Arte Público Press.

Publishes *Folklore and Culture on the Texas-Mexican Border,* University of Texas Press.

1994 Publishes *The Hammon and the Beans, and Other Stories*, consisting of stories written in the 1930s and 1940s, Arte Público Press.

1998 Publishes novella, *The Shadow,* Arte Público Press.

1999 Dies on *Cinco de Mayo* (May 5) in Austin, Texas, on the anniversary of the Mexican defeat of French occupation troops in Puebla, Mexico in 1862.

2002 Américo Paredes Papers opened to the public at the Nettie Lee Benson Latin American Collection.

Preface

This translation of Américo Paredes Manzano's first collection of poetry was undertaken as a collaborative project by Omar Vásquez Barbosa, a former graduate student research assistant at the University of Texas at San Antonio, and me, an Associate Professor of Chicana/o Literature at the same institution. We were a perfect match for this project for several reasons. We are both bilingual and, as published poets, we both have an intimate knowledge of poetry as an art and, above all else, as a difficult, oftentimes tedious, and emotionally taxing craft. This insight has enabled the creativity and perseverance required to reconstruct and, at times, recompose Paredes' varied and sometimes convoluted style and forms of verse.

More importantly, our own personal backgrounds and disciplinary experiences add valuable perspective to the translation process and also provide insights to our overall attempts to produce an aesthetically pleasing and academically useful annotated translation of *Cantos de adolescencia*. That is, in an attempt to introduce this little-known work to a broader audience, we approached Paredes' U.S.-Mexico borderlands poetics from Aztlán (the Southwestern United States) and Latin America, respectively. My own background as a Tejano from a working-class Chicano barrio, along with my comparative literature training in the Department of Spanish and Portuguese at Stanford University and subsequent experience as an English Professor at various universities in the United States, add depth to my firsthand knowledge of the Chicana/o vernacular Spanish and popular culture that is so crucial to Paredes' life and work. My training in Peninsular Spanish Literature as well as my research and writing in Latin American and Chicana/o literatures are crucial to explicating Paredes' poetic discourse, which ranges from the high diction of the Spanish Renaissance to idiomatic Chicana/o Spanish as well as popular poetic and musical forms from the borderlands and the Americas at large. Omar, a *chilango* (Mexico City native) by birth and transplanted Tejano and world traveler, brings a bicultural metropolitan command of the Spanish- and English-languages as well as a corresponding knowledge about Mexican and British literature. In addition, Omar has written several experimental plays that creatively extrapolate from the works of canonical British authors such as Milton, which has given him insights into the complex process of mimicry and transformation that undergirds Paredes' own work. Moreover, Omar's youthful vitality and consummate love of poetry has helped us keep Paredes' art at the center of this archival recovery project.

In an attempt to collapse, as much as possible, the typically hierarchical faculty/student relationship, we divided this project into several components and tasks in order to equally share the joys as well as the burdens of the overall enterprise. Based on our experiences with and research on translation theory and practice, we developed a multiple-stage method that facilitated the task of translating Paredes' manuscript. We began the translation, chronologically from first to last poem, by first producing our own individual translation draft of the piece at hand. We then compared each individual draft and used them as templates to produce a jointly authored working English version of the Paredes original. This joint translation session ranged in time, from thirty minutes to as much as two hours for one draft of a single poem, depending on the complexity and difficulty of the piece. The difficulty oftentimes was compounded by Paredes' colloquialisms and neologisms as well as his frequent use of rhymed verse, irregular rhyme schemes, and highly convoluted

Spanish syntax. After completing jointly authored drafts of the entire manuscript, we approached our translations anew as poets for a third round of revision to make sure that each piece had its own internal integrity while still remaining true to the original. The fourth round of revision involved a joint re-reading of the whole manuscript. We both made minor revisions as appropriate. This was followed by further review, discussion, and collaborative revision via email after Omar returned to Mexico City and then moved to Spain to pursue a career in filmmaking. Finally, we decided to bring closure to the draft stage of the project after eighteen months in order to solicit feedback from outside readers. I then made one more review and revision of the entire manuscript in light of this feedback and submitted the penultimate version to Dr. Nicolás Kanellos, Director of Arte Público Press and the Recovering the U.S. Hispanic Literary Heritage Project. Final adjustments were made to the overall document in consultation with the editors of Arte Público Press.

Unlike the translation regimen, which we shared, we divided the research component of the project into individual tasks. I was responsible for initiating the project and writing all grants for support. We received several awards: a Faculty Research Grant awarded to me by the University of Texas at San Antonio in 1992 to conduct preliminary research and plan the project, a Grant-In-Aid from the Recovering the U.S. Hispanic Literary Heritage Project, which was awarded to Omar and me for the translation portion, and a Research Assistantship awarded to us both from the UTSA Department of English, Classics and Philosophy to continue the project. I conducted all the archival recovery research at the Archival Collections room at the Benson Latin American Collection at the University of Texas at Austin, where I searched for and reproduced Paredes' manuscript and relevant loose poems, correspondence, related writings, and photographs. Omar conducted research to trace Paredes' eclectic invocations of British, Spanish, French, and classical Greek literature and folklore. This involved extensive study of poetry from a variety of literary figures that include Gustavo Adolfo Bécquer, Lord Alfred Tennyson, Algernon Charles Swinburne, Ben Jonson, and John Keats among many others. Omar also conducted musicology research to help define and describe the folk music forms that Paredes glosses, and he also provided etymologies and taxonomies to explain obscure references that frequently emerged in Paredes' verse (e.g., the *zenzontli* bird). We both worked together to track down other interpersonal and intertextual references, which ranged from former Mexican expatriate cultural arts patron Nemesio García Naranjo to Paredes contemporaries such as the obscure young Mexican-American poet Roberto Ramírez Ramírez.

We used the resultant data to complete the annotations and addenda and also to jointly author the introduction. I was responsible for researching and writing the first part of the introduction on Paredes' significance to Chicana/o and American cultural studies, and Omar was responsible for researching and writing the second section regarding the different schools of translation theory and practice. We jointly reviewed and revised the overall draft of the introduction. As the Director of the Américo Paredes Translation Project I took editing license to complete the final draft of the entire manuscript for submission to Arte Público Press. While I am the founder and director of the Américo Paredes Translation Project, we both share authorship and equal copyright for the manuscript.

B.V. Olguín, Director
Américo Paredes Translation Project

Acknowledgments

Many people are responsible for the publication of this translation of Américo Paredes Manzano's inaugural collection of verse. The project had its genesis in an invitation made to Ben by Professor José Limón, Director of the Center for Mexican American Studies at the University of Texas at Austin. He was asked to make a presentation at the first annual Américo Paredes symposium in 2001, and became aware of the existence of *Cantos de adolescencia* during the research for the presentation. Ben's presentation, incidentally, was the only one devoted to Paredes' verse, which illuminated the need for greater access to this text. University of Texas at Austin Professor Emiliano Zamora provided enthusiastic encouragement for the translation project.

Ben received a grant from the College of Liberal and Fine Arts at the University of Texas at San Antonio (UTSA) to conduct preliminary archival research in 2002, which resulted in a research article in *Aztlán* published in the 30th Anniversary Special Issue in 2005. Both Ben and Omar received a grant to begin translating the book from the Recovering the U.S. Hispanic Literary Heritage Project. The Department of English, Classics and Philosophy at UTSA also provided generous support to the translation team by awarding Ben and Omar with a Research Assistantship to continue with the project. We thank these agencies and programs for their support.

The archivists at the Benson Latin American Collection ensured the success of the project. Margot Gutiérrez was helpful throughout the entire process and the entire staff of the Archival Collections and Rare Book Room were absolutely wonderful. Their proficient help in locating relevant materials, including those that are not part of the Américo Paredes Papers, was invaluable. Moreover, their enthusiasm for research was contagious and inspiring and motivated the completion of the project that, after the first one hundred hours of archival research, had became quite tedious even as it was always thrilling to watch a literary life unfold page by page.

This project to translate the early poetry of a foundational figure in Chicana/o literary history also relied on the research of distinguished Paredes scholars such as Ramón Saldívar, José David Saldívar, Rafael Pérez-Torres, María Herrera-Sobek, José Limón, Hector Perez, Rachel Jennings, and Louis G. Mendoza. John M. González introduced Ben to the possibility of Chicano signifying in Paredes' verse during a bus ride several days after the 2001 Paredes Symposium that, incidentally, was stopped by the U.S. Border Patrol. We offer the Immigration and Naturalization (INS) officers who interrogated them a bit of gratitude for reminding us that the colonial context that Paredes engaged in the 1930s is still an intrusive and oppressive part of the Chicana/o reality today. As an addendum to the forced response to the INS query of "where were you born," we note that the "here" they referenced is the geopolitical terrain Don Américo called Nuevo Santander to the day he died. We call it Aztlán.

UTSA Professors Wendy Barker and Norma Cantú provided Omar with invaluable mentoring in creative writing and also helped inspire his interests in poetry and translation.

We are particularly grateful for early readings of the manuscript by UTSA Professors Louis G. Mendoza, Norma Cantú, Santiago Daydí-Tolson, and Bernadette Andrea. Professor Barker also provided crucial insights on overcoming some translation challenges in the preface to her jointly authored translation of Rabindranath Tagore, which served as a model for our project. The staff of the College of Liberal and Fine Arts at the

UTSA Downtown Campus, especially Sylvia Rodriguez and David Espinoza, provided crucial technical and logistical support. This project simply could never have been completed without their patience and solidarity. More importantly, the college also helped defray costs for printing, phone calls, postage, and materials related to the research and writing. We offer a special thanks to former UTSA Dean Louis Mendoza for taking a personal interest in the project and his continued solidarity and consultations from his new post as the Director of the Chicana/o Studies Department at the University of Minnesota.

Finally, Dr. Nicolás Kanellos deserves another thanks for his diligent support of broader efforts to recuperate and publish Paredes' early works. This project, like so much of the relatively new discipline of Chicana/o literary studies, is indebted to Kanellos' vision, diligence, and overall commitment to Raza Letters. He is an unsung hero who gave many Chicana and Chicano writers their start by publishing their works when no one would even read their writing. Moreover, Kanellos continues his trailblazing mission to expand and diversify the conventional understanding about the literatures of the Americas by also enabling us to recover the unread works by major Chicana/o authors. Un abrazo.

B.V. Olguín and Omar Vásquez Barbosa

Introduction

Reconstructing Chicana/o Literary History: Américo Paredes Manzano & the Foundations of Pocho Poetics

¡Soy pocho! Dios me haga	I'm Pocho! May God make me
orgullo de los pochos	pride of the Pochos
así como los pochos son	just like Pochos are
mi orgullo.	my pride.
Quisiera llegar a ser	I would like to become
el orgullo de los pochos.	the pride of Pochos.
	—Américo Paredes, circa 1940

I. Recovering Paredes

When Américo Paredes wrote this short limerick in his mid twenties, he could never have guessed that he not only would become the "pride" of Mexican Americans—the proverbial Pochos—but also a model for subsequent generations of Mexican-American and Chicana/o poets and artists.[1] (See Figure 1.) In fact, by the time of his death on the symbolically significant day of May 5, 1999 at the age of 84, he had become an icon in the relatively new discipline of Chicana/o Studies. Even before he wrote these playful though ultimately prophetic words, the young Paredes (who followed the Mexican custom of using his mother's maiden name "Manzano" until he entered the U.S.

Army in 1944), already had published dozens of newspaper editorials and features on Mexican-American culture and politics, composed songs in English and Spanish, and written three collections of poetry in English, Spanish and vernacular bilingual combinations of both.[2] He succeeded in publishing one of these manuscripts, the Spanish-language anthology he titled *Cantos de adolescencia*, which was issued through Librería Española in 1937 in San Antonio, Texas. (See Figure 2.) These published and unpublished early writings, which became available to the public through the Américo Paredes Papers at the Archival Collections of the Nettie Lee Benson Latin American Collection at the University of Texas at Austin in 2002, are among Paredes' least known yet perhaps most important works: they foreground many of the concerns that will crystalize in the succeeding fifty years of Paredes' multi-facetted career as a poet, short story writer, novelist, folklorist, musicologist, and literary scholar. Paredes' eclectic and wide-ranging corpus of creative and scholarly writings is particularly important because it anticipates—and some say inaugurates—Chicana/o literary and cultural studies as an academic discipline in the 1970s and 1980s. The ever-growing number of articles, books, theses, and dissertations about Paredes' writings is testament to his stature as the "Mexican American W.E.B. Du Bois." Indeed, Paredes' extended explorations of the Pocho, whom he proposed as the paradigmatic bicultural yet bifurcated Mexican-American subject with his own unique vernacular epistemology can be seen as a U.S.-Mexico borderlands analogue to Du Bois' "double consciousness."[3]

Despite the popularity of Paredes' scholarship, his own literary work, especially his poetry, only recently has begun to receive the critical attention it deserves. However, with the exception of B.V. Olguín's recent article in the Chicano Studies Journal, *Aztlán*, all studies of Paredes' poetry have been based exclusively on his second collection of verse, *Between Two Worlds*, which was co-edited by Ramón Saldívar in 1991.[4]

While it is important to note that *Between Two Worlds* includes a significant number of poems that span 1934 to 1971 (including selections from Paredes' early aborted poetry collections we discuss further below), it excludes all but one poem from Paredes' *Cantos de adolescencia.* This poem—the original 1934 English version of "The Rio Grande" that the author had recomposed in Spanish in 1936 as "El Río Bravo" for inclusion in his inaugural Spanish-language collection—serves as a bridge between both anthologies. More importantly, this poem about a river with two names that functions as a border also serves as a metonym of Paredes' conflicted, life-long preoccupation with place, language, and the complexities of Mexican-American literary and cultural genealogy. Even though Paredes knew *what* he wanted to write about at this formative period in his life—the turbulent history of the lower Rio Grande/Río Bravo borderlands and its people's defiant and resilient longevity—he was not completely sure of which language and style to use and, moreover, what it all meant. His subsequent life-long efforts to explicate the unique elements of Mexican-American life are first illustrated in *Cantos de adolescencia*, which encompasses the short but crucial period from 1932-1937, when the poet grew from a seventeen-year-old adolescent to a twenty-one-year-old young man. More importantly, the poems in Paredes' first collection not only foreground the attributes that scholars have celebrated in their examinations of *Between Two Worlds*. Rather, they illustrate how Paredes' apparent diatribes against U.S. imperialism and purported celebrations of cultural hybridity are more ideologically inchoate; so much so that they may require a complete paradigm shift in Chicana/o literary and cultural studies.

Scholars of Paredes' prose have noted that his innovative hybrid poetics and provocative counterhegemonic posture revolve around the conflicted spatial ontology of the borderlands Mexico-Texan, which Paredes frequently referred to as the Pocho.[5] The Pocho emerges as a historical archetype in the

U.S.-Mexico borderlands as a result of the shift to U.S. hegemony following the American annexation of the region at the culmination of the U.S.-Mexico War in 1848. This figure generally is understood to be an acculturated person of Mexican descent born (or raised) in the conflicted border region that is renowned for Mexico-Texan insurrection and attendant Anglo-Texan atrocities. Like Homi Bhabha's mimic man, the Pocho's deliberate attempts to claim inclusion in the polis ironically mark his exclusion due in part to a lingering accent, cultural mistranslations, and transformations, as well as other signifiers of difference such as dark skin. It is therefore not surprising that the Pocho has become a stock figure in Mexican-American and Chicana/o literature who animates competing ideologies. In depictions by many Mexican and even Mexican-American authors prior to the 1950s, the Pocho serves as a Mexican-American model of cultural degeneracy for his or her purported loss of "Mexicanness" arising from life in the United States. In contrast, the literature of the Chicana/o civil rights era during the 1960s and 1970s oftentimes represents the Pocho as an idealized racial and cultural "mestizo" (mixed-blood subject), or rather, the empowered Chicana/o. Paredes' lifelong work resists such simplistic binaries and *Cantos de adolescencia* is crucial to his exploration of the complexities of Mexican-American hybridity.

Paredes first articulates a portrait of this paradigmatic figure through intimate, oftentimes painful personal expressions of angst and analysis in the pages of his adolescent and young adult verse. Indeed, of all the forms and genres Paredes utilized—from scholarly prose, various song genres in English and Spanish, editorial and feature journalism, and prose fiction—poetry remains the only genre in which Paredes allowed himself the liberty to indulge in the first person voice to explore the themes that make him such an important figure in Chicana/o Studies and broader American Studies. It is fitting, then, that one of the titles Paredes considered for a collection to accompany *Cantos de adolescencia* was "Alma Pocha," or "Pocho Soul," which also was the title of an expanded version of his 1936 poem "El Pocho."[6] (For versions of these poems, see Addenda.) The "Alma Pocha" remained an important trope in his explorations of Mexican-American epistemology and ontology throughout his multi-genre corpus, and he considered using it again as the title of a proposed collected poems towards the end of his life. (This proposed collection subsequently was retitled as *Various Verse*, then *Versos varios* and, finally, was published in abbreviated form as *Between Two Worlds*.) The *alma pocha* ultimately becomes the signifier of a unique persona and poetic that helped define an important rupture and genesis in the literature of the Americas. That is, as early as the 1930s Paredes names *and* performs what subsequent generations of scholars of Mexican-American and Chicana/o poetry such as Alfred Arteaga later will identify as a complex "intercultural heteroglot" signifying practice composed of competing and conflicting genealogies that nonetheless retains its own integrity as a unique poetic (1994, 13). This Pocho poetic is dramatically rendered in Paredes' first person, autobiographical poetic persona throughout the pages of *Cantos de adolescencia*, and therefore makes this text an indispensable touchstone for all Paredes scholarship as well as Mexican-American and Chicana/o literary studies.

This jointly authored translation and bilingual edition of *Cantos de adolescencia*, which we are calling *Songs of Youth* for reasons discussed further below, is thus intended to serve multiple audiences. First and foremost, we have sought to present an accurate and poetically accomplished translation, that is, a translation that retains the integrity of the Spanish original while still reading as good poetry in English. (We have been aided in this endeavor in several cases by Paredes' own English versions that have been recovered from the Américo Paredes Papers as well as by the original English poems he glosses from poets such as Ben Jonson.) An English translation of this foundational figure in Mexican-American Letters, we hope, will expand

Paredes' audience and also enable his large number of bilingual and monolingual fans to access the works from his important formative period. This translation and related annotations also are intended for a scholarly audience interested in further exploring Paredes' discourses on hybridity, cultural conflict, transnationalism, gender relations, race relations, materialism, and the variety of other topics he engages in his later works. This translation is particularly essential to Paredes scholarship given that it provides primary materials from the author's adolescence and young adulthood—which he calls the period of "transition" and "metamorphosis"—that has remained unexamined and undertheorized in all extant biographies and related scholarship. Moreover, *Cantos de adolescencia* includes poems from as early as 1932, two years before the earliest poem included in *Between Two Worlds*, and several years before Paredes commenced his now canonical historical novel, *George Washington Gómez* in 1936.[7] We also provide facsimiles of select early poems, including Paredes' earliest extant poem from 1930, when the poet was not yet 15, as well as other loose poems up to 1937, the publication date of *Cantos de adolescencia*. (See Figures 5 and 9.) This text thus can be seen as a complement to, and extension of *Between Two Worlds*. To further aid readers and researchers, we also include a facsimile of Paredes' own Table of Contents for a planned collection, which references some poems that are now lost. (See Figure 59.) In some cases, we also have included facsimiles of poems written after 1937 in order to situate important issues, themes, and signifying practices in Paredes' literary corpus.

We recognize that this endeavor to recuperate and reconstruct the legacy of a poet after his death is highly problematic, especially given the fact that Paredes personally and deliberately destroyed many of his early poems so that they never would be published. However, we take these recovery, translation, and publication liberties with implicit license from Don Américo Paredes himself. In a typed log in which he itemizes his preparation of his personal papers for archiving—a process that also included the permanent destruction of as many as several dozen poems—Paredes recognizes the importance of his early verse even as he expresses dissatisfaction with their quality. In the entry dated April 16, 1979, he writes:

> [I] began sifting through my verse today, with the intention of throwing away a good part and saving some that may be left behind me. Twenty years or so ago, my intention had been to destroy almost all of it. I am aware that most of it is incredibly bad, especially the verse in English; and that even the better pieces are not especially memorable. Still, since every one of my verbal atrocities has sentimental and biographical value for me, I put off the holocaust until I should be closer to the end. But things have changed in the past decade. During that time I have become a "Precursor" to the young Mexicanos in Texas and California. My literary attempts, no matter their quality, have become of historical interest to them. Already Alurista has published a few of my verse compositions in Spanish; and María Herrera-Sobek, my first "biographer," has even dug up that folly of my youth, *Cantos de adolescencia*, and commented upon it in an article she has done on me for a forthcoming dictionary of Chicano scholars and writers.[8]

Towards the end of the entry that later forms the basis of the prologue to the aforementioned planned (but never published) anthology of collected poems, *Versos varios*, he turns his historicist cultural studies gaze onto his own writings:

> Furthermore, the content of many of the verse compositions—even the very bad ones—do reveal something about my feelings and attitudes during the 1930s and 1940s on such things as racial relations and culture conflict. These are the things young Mexicanos are asking me about these days. So I will try to make some notes about things as I saw them (as they are recorded in some of the discarded pieces) for somebody's future reference, perhaps even mine.

Apparently aware of his status as a precursor to Chicano cultural nationalist poets, Paredes makes a point of recording the titles of all his poems. He also summarizes their content and even excerpts those he destroyed:

> I will leave a record of themes and titles of the pieces discarded for purposes of remembering landmarks of years past. I may even have time to write down something in the way of memoirs. If not, they may be grist for some Chicano scholar's mill later on.[9]

The translations and related annotations included in this bilingual volume thus are intended to further the cause to which Paredes dedicated the greater part of his own life: the continued production of knowledge about Mexican Americans and Chicana/os. Paredes' early poetry is invaluable grist for this mill. We thank him for this gift.

As such, this translation of *Cantos de adolescencia* fulfills the stated goals of the Arte Público Press Recovering the U.S. Hispanic Literary Heritage Project, which sponsored the enterprise. Under the direction of noted scholar Nicolás Kanellos, Arte Público Press' groundbreaking initiative received funding by the Rockefeller Foundation to undertake the enormous task of locating, rescuing, evaluating, and disseminating "primary literary materials written by Hispanics, from the colonial period to 1960, across the geographic area that is now the United States."[10] To date, scholars sponsored by this initiative have recovered literally thousands of novels, memoirs, treatises, plays, poetry anthologies, and assorted other writings produced by Latinas/os in the area that subsequently becomes the United States of America dating as far back in history as the sixteenth century. Recovery Project scholars also have published nearly a dozen recovered texts and produced over 100 scholarly articles and presentations. Pursuant to recovering, translating and annotating *Cantos de adolescencia*, and further illuminating its author's significance to Mexican-American literary and cultural history—which is an inalienable part of the literary and cultural history of the Americas in general—we have included relevant excerpts of correspondence, photographs, and other materials from the Américo Paredes Papers. These include the original advertisement for *Cantos de adolescencia*, which cost $1 in 1937, or "$4 Oro Nacional," that is, four Mexican Pesos linked to the gold standard. (See Figure 3.) We also include selected newspaper clippings and correspondence announcing the precocious young poet's performances as well as his numerous awards from 1932 to the early 1940s. (See Figures 4-15.) The archives contain an even more important document: the badly deteriorated yet still legible October 18, 1937 issue of the Spanish-language newspaper *La Prensa* (San Antonio, Texas), which ran a two-page pull-out that features *Cantos de adolescencia*. (See Figure 16.)

This addition to the Recovering the U.S. Hispanic Literary Heritage Project also contains facsimiles of the original published versions of the poems that comprise *Cantos de adolescencia* as well as those from the same period that are excluded from the manuscript. Many of the prefaces to these early poems provide significant contextual notes by the author or newspaper editor. The poem "Guadalupe la Chinaca," for instance, was used to advertise a major musical performance by a prominent Mexican singer. (See Figures 17-18.) Like other occasional poems that Paredes published, such as "New Year's Eve," this advertisement reveals his role as a populist oral bard whose literary productions and performances were undertaken for the purpose of being both utilitarian and entertaining for a mass audience. (See Figure 19.) In fact, the oral bard is a popular and common figure in Mexican-American and Chicana/o poetry up to the present.[11] This apparently trite populist poetic also was very serious and politically engaged. On this note, the prefaces to Paredes' 1935 biting anti-imperialist satirical and existentialist poem, "The Mexico-Texan," offer several unexpected insights into the various negotiations of power by several segments of the Mexican-American population during the 1930s. In the introductory comments to a previously unknown Spanish version of the poem published in *La Voz*, a Spanish-language newspaper in Brownsville, Texas, the editor asks "pardon of our Mexico-Texan readers who are sufficiently intelligent enough to know how to take the humorous tone of the composition."[12] In an English reprint of the poem in another South Texas newspaper, the editors justify their publication of the poem by citing from a statement issued by the League of United Latin American Citizens (LULAC), which apparently was the first to publish Paredes' verse explication of the brutal psychological toll of U.S. imperialism on Mexican Americans. In a position that seems uncharacteristic of the otherwise strategically patriotic organization, LULAC proclaimed: "We published this rhyme because it contains more truth than poetry and everyone who reads it will know how to understand its merit."[13] In the *Brownsville Herald* publication of a longer English version, Paredes notes that the poem "was never meant for publication," but adds that since it apparently had been circulating in altered bootlegged forms and was even being used for political rallies, he chose to publish the poem in its original form. He adds, perhaps with too much hyperbole to be taken at face value, that the poem was nothing but "a whim of a half-serious, half-comic mood."[14] (For facsimiles of early publications of "The Mexico-Texan" see Figures 20-22.) Together, these facsimiles shed light on the early popular reception of a figure whose writings were responding to the popular and populist needs and sentiments of the South Texas Mexican-American population long before the publication of his more renowned work, *With His Pistol in His Hand: A Border Ballad and Its Hero* in 1958.

In addition to these materials, we include facsimiles of selected letters by newspaper editors that laud the young author's literary merit. In one significant instance, the editor of *El Regional*, a Spanish-language periodical in the Mexican border town of Matamoros (for which Paredes later worked), was so impressed with *Cantos de adolescencia* that he called the poems that comprise it "early poetic fruits of magnificent taste," and urged the novice writer to try his hand at prose. One can only imagine how such glowing praise from an esteemed editor influenced the young Paredes, especially since he dates his first novel, *George Washington Gómez,* as having been initiated in 1936 and completed in 1940. The archives also contain letters of praise from the noted University of Texas librarian Carlos E. Castañeda. Paredes even engaged in correspondence with the *Texas Farming and Citriculture Journal*, an unlikely venue that published his poetry. The young Paredes, it seems, was as diligent in promoting his writing as he was at producing it. (See Figures 23-26.) A less provocative though no less interesting item in the Américo Paredes Papers is the original leather jacket awarded to Paredes by the prestigious journal, *The Arizona Quarterly*, in recognition of the literary merit he exhibits in *Cantos de adolescencia*. The colorful jacket fit perfectly. (See Figure 27.) The archive collection also contains one of the three known copies of the original *Cantos de adolescencia*, in which Paredes included a stunning photograph of himself dressed as a Pachuco that we have recuperated for the cover of this translation.[15] We also have included an equally significant photograph of Paredes as a young boy alongside his sister Blanca on the occasion of her first communion. Blanca apparently died as a young girl and Paredes dedicated several poems to her, such as "A Blanca," which is part of *Cantos de adolescencia*. (See Figures 28-29.)

The wealth of materials contained in the Américo Paredes archives inevitably extends beyond the scope of this translation project but are nonetheless important to recognize. Indeed, in the process of reviewing the extensive archive, which contains over 69 linear feet of printed matter as well as other textile and audiovisual materials, we discovered previously unpublished and unknown poems and related song lyrics. The poems not only date to Paredes' earliest surviving compositions from 1930, but also date to his last known poem, the 1981 poem "Última carta," which the author removed from the final version of *Between Two Worlds* during the final stage of editing.[16] The archives also reveal that Paredes was the consummate poet, oftentimes interspersing poems in personal letters to family, friends, and colleagues. Indeed, most of his correspondence to his wife is imbedded with love poetry. And Paredes was a tireless note taker. His archives contain numerous loose sheets and also more extensive handwritten notebooks with limericks and doggerel verse as well as accomplished first drafts of published poems and completed drafts of compositions that have never been published.

Paredes even was an avid collector of poems from family and, more importantly, the circle of poets from South Texas who wrote voluminous letters and poems that frequently included glosses from each others' compositions. In a June 23, 1989 letter to Nicolás Kanellos, Paredes recalls:

> There were a lot of us *mejicanos* writing verse and prose in the 30s and 40s; I belonged to a little group of such writers on the Lower Border. But as far as I know, I was the only one who attempted to address the social and political problems of our people through literature.[17]

These fellow borderlands poets included multigenerational, trans-border members such as Antonio Arangua, Mariano Manzano, Eleazar Paredes, Jose Peña, Sabas Klahn, Adan Ramos, Oscar J. del Castillo, Roberto Ramírez Ramírez, Gonzalo Casas Gutiérrez, Petronilo M. Preciado, E.M. Cortinas, Francisco Valdez, and Manuel Cruz, whose works have yet to be recovered and analyzed.[18] The correspondence between Paredes and his circle of writers involved poetry critiques and recommended revisions of each others' works. In various letters and poems, for instance, Manuel Cruz provides important critiques on nomenclature (e.g., Paredes' early use of "American" to refer to Anglo Americans instead of Latin Americans at large), and on matters concerning Pocho identity. Paredes incorporates his advice in later writings. In return, Paredes even wrote a prologue for

Cruz' poetry collection *Romanso azul*, a manuscript that is now lost. (The archives contain over 100 letters between Paredes and Cruz.)

The correspondence between circle members also frequently includes *homenajes*, that is, occasional poems celebrating one another's accomplishments or gratuitously celebrating their group as a whole, which included a cadre of young bohemians like Paredes. One example is the poem "*Pasatiempo lírico*" ("Lyrical Pastime") by Manuel Cruz, which apparently recounts one of their frequent bachanalian reunions in 1944. These gatherings apparently span from the mid 1930s into the next decade and correspondence continued until the deaths of the circle members. Furthermore, many of these poets dedicate poems to Américo Paredes, and Paredes repays the favor with *homenajes*, or tributes, to them up to the late 1950s. Indeed, even as late as the 1950s, Paredes uses a poem from a friend in a love letter to his wife Amelia. Moreover, several of his poems in *Cantos de adolescencia* contain glosses of poems written by members of what can veritably be called the lower Rio Grande Writer's Circle, the term we use to refer to this cohort. The archives also contain several poems from Paredes' father Eleazar Paredes and relatives such as Mariano Manzano (who were members of the group), as well as some youthful compositions that apparently are from a son. Rubén Paredes Cantú, another cousin, also dedicated a *décima* to Paredes as late as 1982.[19] The Manzano and Paredes clans, the archives suggest, might be considered nascent Tejano literary families in a region rich with as yet unrecognized and unrecovered literary talent. (See Figures 30-45.) This literary recovery work remains to be done.

A more vexing problem introduced by the Américo Paredes Papers concerns the author's blurring of genres. Paredes is renowned for his recovery and preservation of vernacular forms of discourse and genres such as the epic heroic corrido. In fact, his primary claim to fame is his aforementioned archeology of "El corrido de Gregorio Cortez" ("The Ballad of Gregorio

Cortez"), which forms the basis of *With His Pistol in His Hand: A Border Ballad and Its Hero* (1958), and a related feature film directed by Robert Young, *The Ballad of Gregorio Cortez* (1984). Paredes' early works, however, reveal his experiments with Greek, English, Anglo-American, Mexican, and Mexican-American genres and signifying practices that make him, as an artist, much harder to fix within any single genealogy. For instance, he freely experiments with traditional forms such as Greek fables, European sonnets, and Spanish and Mexican *décimas* as well as folk song genres such as the *son*, *danzón*, *bolero,* and *tango*, among others. (The archives even contain examples of haikus and very many *dichos*, or vernacular proverbs, that Paredes apparently developed himself.) Adding to his complicated galley of influences, newspaper clippings in the Américo Paredes Papers reveal that his earliest literary awards were for Petrarchan Sonnets! Moreover, as illustrated by the cover to the original edition of *Cantos de adolescencia*, Paredes' poetic sensibilities are informed by classical models and Orientalist discourses. His poem "Fábula" is exemplary for its mimetic invocation of classical Greek fables, which he studied as part of his classicist training at UT Austin. The allusions to Pan on the cover illustration becomes particularly significant because it provides a contrapuntal model of the "search for roots" paradigm that later generations of Chicana/o authors will find in Mesoamerica. The irony arises from the fact that scholars have situated Paredes as a precursor to Chicana/o cultural nationalism. Moreover, the enormous and apt critical attention paid to Paredes' anti-imperialist discourse also must be situated alongside the seemingly benign yet nonetheless exoticized image of an Arabian lamp on the cover of his first book, and the more problematic images of exotic foreign women in his later poetry that usually accompany such allusions in Western literature. As Olguín has explicated in his aforementioned essay, these highly racialized and gendered transnational allusions threaten to destabilize Paredes' panamericanist and internationalist discourses precisely because he replicates imperialist fantasies of the exotic Other. More critical work needs to be conducted into these contradictory and complicated aspects of Paredes' work. The question of genealogy and genre is made even more fascinating given that Paredes set many of his lyrics to music or wrote lyrics for music he previously had written. We have featured selections of the original lyrics and scores for selected poems/songs included in *Cantos de adolescencia* (See Figures 46-48).

This blurring of genres across literary traditions, which perhaps may also be seen as Paredes' recognition of the oral roots of all poetry, may even necessitate a reassessment of previous celebrations of Paredes as a precursor to Chicana/o cultural nationalism, as well as more critical interrogation of the complicated and contradictory nature of cultural nationalism in general. The Prologue to *Cantos de adolescencia*, in which the author proclaims his collection to be the culmination of his decision to never again write in English, actually reveals a conflict over language and related literary influences that not only preoccupies Paredes for the rest of his life and career, but continues to animate debates among subsequent generations of Mexican American and Chicana/o writers and critics up to the present:

> *Los años desde 1930 hasta 1936 forman una etapa de transición en mi vida—son los años ciegos y desequilibrados de metamórfosis . . . [El niño] se sintió un momento netamente mexicano y al otro puro yanqui. Pero con la adolescencia llega el tiempo de las decisiones.*
>
> *Estas páginas son el resultado de esta lucha en el tiempo de decisión. Comencé a escribir verso desde la edad de quince años pero mis obras fueron todas en inglés. Mis versos en español no comienzan hasta en 1932, dos años después. Esto se debe a la influencia de una escuela en inglés y de muy pocos libros en la lengua de Cervantes. En verdad, todavía me siento más seguro de mí mismo en la lengua de Shakespeare que en la mía. (3)*

As the proliferation of later English compositions in *Between Two Worlds* confirms, Paredes never truly resolves his linguistic dilemma: he continues to compose in both languages and a vernacular hybridization of both that ultimately comes to characterize Pocho poetics. Moreover, an existentialist trajectory evolves within Paredes' poetry corpus; it is a crisis that is at once inflected through his conflicted Mexican-American identity but also occasioned by the horrors of World War II. The sonnet dedicated to Manuel Cruz in his letter dated January 7, 1943 is a prime example of a feature that Limón has identified as "Paredes' tragic sentiment of the world." (See Figure 37.) Other archival notes and limericks add to this under-examined aspect of Paredes' poetics. (See Figures 49-50.) Chicana/o existentialism and its relationship to post-WWI existentialism is perhaps a new avenue of inquiry that *Cantos de adolescencia* and Paredes' other early writings may enable. In a further twist on an already complicated genealogy, the archives also reveal that during his nearly one-decade-long sojourn in Asia with the U.S. Army and the American Red Cross, Paredes even tried his hand at composing poems in phonetic Japanese! (See Figures 51-53.)

This linguistic and existentialist dilemma is foregrounded in a paradigmatic performance of colonial mimicry as a young boy that enables us to further situate *Cantos de adolescencia* in a specific time and place even as we continue to decenter the Chicana/o cultural nationalist chauvinism it inaugurates. In the April 17, 1979 entry to the aforementioned log, Paredes recalls:

> Looking over these old papers, I was reminded of my first "poem" in English, composed when I was in the third grade with Miss McCollum, bless her soul where she or it may be. I remember her very kindly. Time: the 1924-25 school year; I was nine. Miss McCollum read it in class, and I was very proud. I suppose it was then that I decided that I would be a poet in the English language, and it would be many years before I would stop trying. I still remember the four-line bit of doggerel, but I will not leave it recorded here. It was about a

little pony I rode all over the countryside and across the river deep and wide.[20]

Even though he qualifies his mimetic desires by discussing the colonialist context—his archives contain writings in which he complains about his teachers' racism and incompetence—he also recounts how he actually loves European literature, especially the literature of Spain and England. In the April 18 entry he recalls:

> [Algernon Charles] Swinburne and Gustavo Adolfo Bécquer were my models in those days. And also John Keats and Antonio Plaza. At least, some of my Spanish models were related to real life. My problem in English communication was that I was going through a period of violent nationalistic reaction against the local Anglo culture, which was of course American. At the same time, I was in love with English literature, but that literature was of another place and time—England of the 18th and early 19th centuries, plus Shakespeare and bits of Chaucer and Milton. This was the curriculum of the freshman and sophomore years in junior college, and it was exactly to my liking. In high school I had read Longfellow, Poe, Emerson, Bryant; but I had not been able to understand Whitman. And the bored, gum-chewing sweater girl who was my high-school English teacher was not much help. I do not believe I ever read a serious 20th-century author, especially the American ones until I had been out of school for several years (around 1939); and about the same time I discovered Whitman for myself.
>
> Consequently, the verse in BLACK ROSES [the unpublished and mostly lost manuscript that predates *Cantos de adolescencia*] for the most part used an idiom far removed from that of the U.S. in the 1930s. Complicating matters still further was the fact that most of the pieces were written to or for a daughter of the "enemy."[21]

Paredes' placement of the term "enemy" in quotation marks reveals his awareness that the dilemma over Mexican-American literary genealogy and cultural heritage is never completely resolved in his life—even as late as 1979. (The matter is further complicated by his own interracial second marriage to Amelia Nagamine, a Uruguayan women of Japanese descent to whom he writes some of the most romantic love letters and poems since Pablo Neruda's *Twenty Poems of Love*.) *Cantos de adolescencia*, and the poems written during this formative period, thus pressure for an important paradigm shift in conventional histories of Chicana/o studies that invoke Paredes' presumed cultural nationalist fetish on all things Mexican. They reveal that the early Américo Paredes—who identifies himself as the "proto Chicano" in the preface to *Between Two Worlds*—actually was an Anglophile! Indeed, in the subsection of *Cantos de adolescencia* subtitled "La comedia del amor" ("The Comedy of Love"), Paredes even ventured on a translation of Ben Jonson's 1616 version of the poem "Song: To Celia"—which he then signed as his own! He extended this cross-racial and transnational poetic mimicry with Lord Alfred Tennyson's famous 1889 poem "Crossing the Bar." In the more conventional accounts of Chicana/o literary history, scholars emphasize a dialogue with Spanish-language influences and, in the case of Alurista and other renowned Chicana/o cultural nationalist poets from the 1960s and 1970s Chicana/o Movement era, with Mesoamerica, specifically the Nahuatl poets of the Aztec empire.[22] Paredes' contrapuntal engagement with the British and Spanish literary canons—which he claims to love even as he identified this love as a function of U.S. imperialism—forces us to further assess the oftentimes effaced relationship between Mexican-American literature and the European and Euroamerican traditions. Paredes's literary influences further extends between such canonical poles as British author Thomas Hardy (1840-1928) to more populist authors such as New York born poet Odgen Nash (1902-1971) and Mexican national poet Antonio Plaza (1833-1882). This is a discussion that continues to this day, and Paredes' own negotiations of language, genealogy, and identity—all of which takes shape in his early poetry—enables new insights into a period of Mexican-American literature that has been undertheorized through generational or oppositional "resistance" models.[23] To make matters even more complicated, the Américo Paredes Papers contain drafts for presumably anti-colonialist stories that are drafted on U.S. military stationary![24] As such, *Cantos de adolescencia* offers broader opportunities for providing more complex and accurate assessments of Mexican-American and Chicana/o literature.

This struggle over the appropriate language for Mexican-American literature also is illustrated by the very publication history of *Cantos de adolescencia* and related early works that ultimately were aborted. In this regard, the proposed titles have a metonymic significance. In the aforementioned log entry dated April 17, 1979, in which Paredes recalls that his first poem ever written was a short "four-line bit of doggerel" in English, he also fondly recalls his talent in the rhymed verbal joustings common among borderlands communities that is akin to the African-American rhyming duels known as the "dozens":

> In Spanish, I had been composing quatrains long before this time, though they were not of the type one's teacher would read in class. The boys' verbal dueling tradition I grew up in required the improvisation of insulting quatrains, sometimes sung, and I began doing this sort of thing at an early age, of course.[25]

Nonetheless, his first collection was to be an English anthology entitled *Black Roses*, which was to encompass the period of his life from 1930 to 1936 (ages 15-21). (This title also appears to be an allusion to the poem by his cousin Mariano Manzano, which is included as Figure 32.) This English-language collection was to be prefaced with a quote from Algernon Charles Swinburne (1837-1909), a Victorian English poet, and the frontispiece included a black-ink drawing of a woman that alluded both to an American Southern Belle or an English damsel sitting by the window awaiting her suitor.[26] (See Figures 54-57.) Significantly, Paredes notes in his log that this proposed collection mostly consisted of poems written to the aforementioned Anglo woman named Carolyn, whose middle and surnames were abbreviated as "C.D." Her racial identity was further obfuscated later as "Carolina." As noted above, he describes her as "a daughter of the enemy," which is the justification he has for not following through with his publication effort. He later discusses how some of the poems to Carolyn from another proposed collection titled *Cantos a Carolina* (which he identifies as initially consisting of poems written from 1934-36) had pages torn out, he surmises, by his first wife. Interestingly, a later handwritten title page for *Cantos a Carolina* reveals that he continued to write poems to her as late as 1946. (See Figure 58.) The proto-Chicano, it appears, had an Anglo-American muse for the first part of his poetic life. He destroys some of the surviving poems to "Carolina" of his own volition but also allows several to be included in *Between Two Worlds*. That is, from the very beginning, Paredes' poetic efforts—along with certain non-literary pursuits—were bifurcated and ambivalent. Scholarship on Paredes has yet to adequately interrogate his gendered poetics nor his equally complicated language politics, and this edition is offered as an invitation for such analyses.

As noted above, Paredes apparently produced a series Spanish poems contemporaneous with the English language *Black Roses* (his proposed first collection) that he was to title *Alma Pocha*. This collection later becomes *Versos varios*, then *Cadencias* (which alternately is called *Cadences*), and forms the basis of *Between Two Worlds*. In a short essay titled, "Preface To the 1930-1936 English Collection" that was to preface the aborted *Black Roses*, he notes that *Cadencias* closes on May 31, 1936. This collection, much of which was destroyed, also includes some poems that survived to be published in *Cantos de adolescencia*. Most of these are *Rimas*, or Rhymes, which are short oftentimes trite love limmericks inspired by, or direct translations of the Spanish Romantic poet Gustavo Adolfo Bécquer (1836-1870). This preface makes reference to materials that apparently are lost (perhaps even destroyed by the author himself). In a surprising archival discovery, Paredes also refers to a collection of multi-genre writings titled *Nonesensicalities*, which he claims to have written under the pseudonym "Guálinto Gómez"—the epynomous characer in his historical novel *George Washington Gómez*. This link to Paredes' paradigmatic Pocho character, whose heroic name is transformed by the borderlands Spanish accent into Guálinto—a South Texas permutation of Bhabha's "mimic man"—invites further study of the autobiographical basis of the novel even though these writings apparently are lost.[27] This is particularly significant because Guálinto's ambiguous ideological status at the end of the novel seems dissonant with the hypernationalist poems of *Cantos de adolescencia*; that is, Paredes' Pocho, and Paredes-as-Pocho, share a tense relationship with one another that scholars have yet to fully explore. This Preface also references a collection of songs to be called *Musicalities*.[28] In the log entry dated April 15, 1979, he notes that he has successfully transcribed 34 of the 60 songs he once composed or knew, and had planned to continue reconstructing as many as possible in the ensuing years of his life.[29] Some of these songs, which alternately were written in English and Spanish, find their way into *Cantos de adolescencia* as glosses or as exact reprints.

Finally, the Américo Paredes Papers reveal "Between Two Worlds" to be an appropriate title for a selected works even though it is too incomplete to illustrate the poet's simultaneous negotiations with multiple worlds of influences and interests. As Rafael Pérez-Torres aptly notes: "wandering two worlds Paredes's poetry marks how Chicano culture could begin to move among four, perhaps five" (1995, 271). Paredes' search for a title for the collection that becomes *Between Two Worlds* is itself instructive of his contradictory and complex location at the geographic, linguistic, cultural, and ideological interstices. As noted, Paredes originally planned to revive *Alma pocha* as the title, but also considered *Various Verse* and *Versos varios*. When his editor proposed "The Four Freedoms" (after a satyrical poem of the same title that critiques an imperialist speech by Franklin D. Roosevelt in 1941), Paredes quickly settles on a recommendation made by his colleague and fellow South Texas writer, Rolando Hinojosa, who had proposed *Between Two Worlds*, which is a gloss from Matthew Arnold (1822-1888), another Victorian English poet.[30] Paredes' original frontispiece, however, was a far more colorful invocation of book titles from publishing conventions of Early Modern Europe, the era that, ironically, was a major period of European imperialist expansion:

Collection
of
Various Verse
from the
Private Papers of Paredes (A.)
being mainly
A CADASTRE OF CANDID CADENCES
Compiled for Cachination
but also including songs
around which were built
Dreams or Destiny
dreams that have died
but which have left in passing
A NIMBUS OF NOSTALGIA
&
This collection covers the period of my Life
from
Today
back into time to
YESTERDAY
Therefore the collection should be read in the Oriental manner—
from the end backwards.

The last two lines suggest that this piece was imagined after his return from Japan in the 1950s. It also provides a refreshing instance of humor that characterizes Paredes' later work, albeit with an understated satyrical jab that becomes his hallmark in works like *With His Pistol in His Hand*. Finally, the archival existence of several proposed tables of contents for Paredes' poetry collections ultimately reveal the interrelated nature of all his poetry; various poems appear, disappear and reappear throughout his initial planning stages and later attempts to reconstruct his own poetic legacy. This bilingual edition of *Cantos de adolescencia* thus is intended to help reconstruct the early period of Paredes' poetry corpus for the purpose of enabling a fuller appreciation of a figure whose virtues as a poet extend before and beyond the verse collected in *Between Two Worlds* and his other more renowned works.

Translating Paredes

In his groundbreaking recovery and analysis of the epic heroic Mexican corrido about the early twentieth century ranch-hand-cum-fugitive Gregorio Cortez, who is hunted down by the Texas Rangers for killing an Anglo-American sheriff in self-defense, Paredes is careful to address the different versions of the event. He thus includes several variants of the same ballad. His role as a scholar and a cultural translator interested in sharing alternative accounts of historical events required that he acknowledge the many possible ways to present this particular octosyllabic sung verse text. Instead of settling on just one version, he presented all the versions he could find. As translators of Paredes' first collection of poetry, however, we do not have the same luxury, since one of our goals is to present a coherent collection of verse that has its own integrity as poetry. Pursuant to this goal, we have had to make some very hard decisions on what we believe to be the best English version of his Spanish original. In this effort we have been guided by several discussion and debates in the field of translation studies.

The precondition for any viable poetry translation is the recognition that literary translation is an art *and* a craft that cannot be successfully performed through the simple substitution of words. All efforts at poetry translation demand that the translators conduct a close contextual reading of the poems in relation to the collection overall. Translators must have a sound appreciation of the poet's overall corpus and biography. Above all else, the goal of most translators is to recompose the poem at hand so that it becomes a viable work of art in the new host language without losing its affiliation to the original. Indeed, the etymology of translation arises from the Latin root, *translare*, which means to carry out, or transport. That is, translation involves the careful transportation of words across languages. Even something as common and simple as a salutation like "hello" requires careful examination. In Italian, for example, *ciao* and *pronto* both can be used as greetings. But the latter one usually is confined to greetings over the telephone. Thus, the translator must be attuned to context as well. Susan Basnnett explains that languages are linguistic systems and the translator's job is to be acquainted with the dynamics of such systems so the final product reflects as closely as possible the essence of the original text (16). In other words, a translator's work should operate in similar or parallel ways in both linguistic systems.

However, this does not necessarily mean that the connections and consequences of a particular line should match exactly. Every text has a unique integrity and a coherent symbolic system shaped by the author. The translator's task is to understand and attempt to convey all the levels and amalgamations the author is displaying through an accurate equivalent that may or may not involve synonyms. For example, an original word may have a particular connotation in the original language that works parallel with the more superficial meaning but not the more important sublime ones. This is illustrated by the Spanish word *brindar*, which is the title of one of Paredes' unpublished sonnets and also appears in several of his published poems. On the superficial level, *brindar* literally means, "to toast." But it also connotes the meanings of "to offer" or "to share." So, in order to maintain that "essence" the translator must scout the new host language for an equivalent word (or words) that not only convey meaning on a superficial level, but also are able to carry out the original connotations as well.

The translator's diligence and proficiency notwithstanding, a translation always will be an approximation of the original; the best a translator can do is create a work that is as close to the original as possible without degenerating into a simplistic literal analogue devoid of any artistry in the new host language. Gregory Rabassa, the noted translator of Gabriel García Marquez' English editions, points out that "a translation can never equal the original; it can approach it, and its quality can only be judged as to accuracy by how close it gets" (1). This position, in fact, falls squarely between some contemporary debates in the field of translation theory and practice. The twentieth century has been witness to two influential schools of literary translation. In the first half of the century, much of translation theory still relied heavily on the Victorian concepts of translation that revolved around literalness and archaizing. These types of translations emphasized the need to convey the remoteness of the original text. They sought to elevate it as a piece of beauty and therefore avoided deviations from the original structure and language. Henry Wadsworth Longfellow epitomized this school in his translation of Dante when he notes:

> The only merit my book has is that it is exactly what Dante says, and not what the translator imagines he might have said if he had been an Englishman. In other words, while making it rhythmic, I have endeavoured to make it also as literal as a prose translation . . . In translating Dante, something must be relinquished. Shall it be the beautiful rhyme that blossoms all along the line like a honeysuckle on the hedge? It must be, in order to retain something more precious than rhyme, namely, fidelity, truth—the life of the hedge itself . . . The business of a translator is to report what the author says, not to explain what he means; that is the work of a commentator. What an author says and how he says it, that is the problem of the translator.[31]

Modern linguistics has placed this positivist literalist approach under greater scrutiny. Indeed, the relationship between translator and text is now readily recognized as being far more subjective and fluid.

Towards the latter half of the century, translators explored other theoretical models, such as the figural approach. Linguistics gave translators new perspectives on how texts are "transferred." According to Rabassa, the job of the translator is never done and that they must be alert to the various possibilities and meanings that "transferring" a single phrase or word entails. Rabassa lucidly notes: "the translator can never be sure of himself, he must never be. He must always be dissatisfied with what he does because ideally, platonically, there is a perfect solution, but he will never find it. He can never enter into the author's being and even if he could the difference in languages would preclude any exact reproduction" (12). Translators take more figural license in their search for an ever better but always already incomplete approximation. This inevitably means that theoretically there are multiple—if not exponential—options available for each line. The most obvious subjective choice that we have made concerns the title. We have chosen to translate *adolescencia* as "youth" instead of the cognate "adolescence," which has a more medical resonance. However, we use "adolescence" in specific parts of the Prologue when Paredes obviously intends to invoke this meaning, such as the third paragraph in which he discusses the psychological and biological aspects of adolescence. Here, he describes *adolescencia* in terms of a physical phenomenon, that is, a stage in one's biological and social life. However, we chose "youth" for the title because it still enables an allusion to the medical significance as well as the existentialist resonance of the collection overall. Moreover, the collection ends with a poem celebrating his twenty-first birthday, which falls outside adolescence and more into young adulthood.

In this context, Américo Paredes' adolescent and young adult poetry has presented various challenges to us as translators and poets. First, it was imperative that we become acquainted with the author's life and education because it directly and indirectly informed his burgeoning *ars poetica*. The collection displays an incredible array of themes—music, politics, identity, romance, and other concerns. Moreover, as noted above, Paredes oftentimes placed himself at the intersection of competing discourses, genres, and traditions. This complex biographical history has had a profound impact in our attempts to "transport" the meaning of fundamental interrelated words and tropes in his poetic corpus. This is particularly the case with interrelated terms such as *pueblo* (town), *patria* (homeland/country), *tierra* (land), *suelo* (earth/floor/land), and *país* (country). For instance, in his poem "México, la ilusión del continente," Paredes uses *pueblo* not to refer to a town, which is the literal meaning, but to identify his Mexican and Mexican-American people (e.g.,"Viendo la huella que sangrienta traza / mi pueblo, que se arroja hacia el arcano," lines 9-10). Therefore, we translated the lines as: "Looking at the bloody footprints that trace / my people, who throw themselves towards the arcane." On the other hand, in the poem "A Mexico," he remarks: "Yo te canté desde muy niño; / amor por tu suelo muy joven sentí; / mi primera poesía en nuestra lengua/ fue patria, para ti" (lines 1-4). In this poem, *patria* clearly displays a psychological and social bond that goes beyond the simple and literal translation of "country." Here it is closer to signifying "homeland," but it also connotes the *pueblo* as well. Furthermore, the word *patria* carries a female gender in Spanish, which enables him to connote a maternal bond to the land itself, further alluding to the signified human subject of *pueblo*. Yet, it would be inaccurate to translate *patria* as "my people" because the poem, from the title to the last line, is a song to a national entity. Therefore, here we translated the term as "homeland" even though this term cannot portray the literal meaning of the word, "motherland," which is awkward and virtually unused in English due to the neutered valence of English language nouns. In summary, even though we believe our use of "homeland" to be the most accurate and salient version possible in English, we recognize that major connotations available in Spanish are lost.

In yet other translations we used an alternative gender-specific term because the context required it. For example, in the poem "Guadalupe la Chinaca," Paredes once again utilizes *patria* as "homeland," but in this case, he exploits the Spanish gender of the word qualifying *patria* as a long-living one, perhaps even an old woman: "Parece ser el canto de mi vieja / patria herida" (lines 8-9). In this instance, our final transported choice is much easier. We chose "motherland," so that the translated line reads: "It appears to be the song of my old / wounded motherland." Finally, the word *país*, which is commonly translated as "country," presents an interesting scenario for its meaning in his poem "Hymno." Here, the meaning is close to both "motherland" and "homeland": "Canten, ríos, alegres y movidos; / canten, vientos, que mueven el maíz. / Canten todos, en un cantar unidos, / la beldad de mi país" (lines 3-6). However, Paredes' poem asks the reader to draw a mental picture of a land. Consequently, in this case the term has a geographical tint. When placed in context, the word does not invoke any sentimental or maternal bonds as "motherland" does, and it does not reflect the patriotic feel "homeland" does. Therefore, the meaning results in "land," which was our choice. The English version thus reads: "Sing, rivers, moving and merry; / sing, winds, that move the cornfield. / Sing all, in a song of unity, / the beauty of my land." The above examples are only a few of the many instances in which apparently simple signifiers and synonyms ultimately involved complex and irregular translations so the English versions were coherent and virtuous in their own right.

Several other related gender issues permeate Paredes' collection at the linguistic level. First Paredes maintains a male default all throughout. As Olguín (2005) has noted, Paredes' verse is inscribed with masculinist discourses. Paredes is quite careful and deliberate in his gendered use of words, which Spanish, a Romance language, facilitates. For instance, in his poem "Rima (XII)," Paredes refers to God as *niño cruel.* The Spanish language has standardized the male gender as universal, so when the expression "niños" are used, the reader automatically assumes it includes males and females. However, in the context of this poem, it would be safe to assume a male diety, and therefore we translate the icon as: "Cruel child." This does not imply that God is automatically male throughout his collection. When Paredes needs to assign a female gender to a deity or person of royal or exalted status, he does not hesitate. In his poem "Oración," for instance, he refers to the deity as *diosa* (goddess) and *sultana* (sultanness). Paredes is methodical and precise when choosing genders and as translators we sought to respect such assignations because they ultimately illuminate the contours of his gendered discourses.

Another challenging aspect of Paredes' poetics arises from his use of colloquialisms that are largely based on a rural south Texas idiom and vernacular phonetic orthographic practices. Following the "figural" school of translation, we decided to approximate the "feel" of colloquial phrases and words instead of attempting to present literal translations, which in some cases would have been grossly different from the original Spanish signifier. We did so in a variety of ways. Instead of losing the colloquial diction, we took our cue from Paredes' own English colloquial poems. In some cases, the language in poems from *Between Two Worlds* was instructive. For instance, in poems such as "The Mexico-Texan," the poet mimics borderland colloquialisms in various types of Spanglish that give us a model of how his dated Tex-Mex idiom might have sounded. This became an issue in poems such as "No Sias Creido," which in standard Spanish would read "No *seas* creido." The "correct" translation of the title would be "Don't Be Conceited." But in order to capture the oral colloquialism alluded to in the vernacular spelling, we translated the title as "Don' be conceited." Paredes not only displays colloquialisms, but neologisms and vernacular spellings as well. For instance, in his poem "Rima (VII)" he introduces the word *blondos cabellos* referring to his beloved's blonde hairs. However, *rubio* is the more common Spanish term for "blond." Yet another instance of vernacular or archaic spellings occurs in his poem "Ojos tristes," in which Paredes writes: "Corasón, todo le distes, . . . mira el mal que me ficistes" (lines 4,12). The standard spellings would be: "diste," "corazón," and "hiciste." On the one hand, Chicana/o Spanish oftentimes transposes spellings so that *diste* becomes *dites*; thus Paredes' use falls in-between the vernacular and the standard. On the other hand, he uses an "f" for an "h," which is a convention from archaic spellings that did not affect the pronunciation of the "h" sound.

As we encountered Paredes' colloquialisms as well as vernacular terms and spellings, we took great care not to take inordinate liberties for fear of deviating too far from the original. However, in some cases we did deviate from literal translations in order to preserve the rhyme scheme when this was an obvious and important aspect of a poem. In other cases, however, we had no acceptable option for maintaining the original essence except by leaving particular words in their original Spanish. For example, in his poem "Canciones," he lists various Latin American songs that have come to be known worldwide by their original name such as *rumbas*, *corridos*, and *sones*. (We have provided descriptions and definitions of these forms and genres in the annotations following relevant poems.) So, by keeping their Spanish names, the musicality is not altered. We are guided in this practice by Wendy Barker's discussion of a similar translation problem she encountered with the Bengali word *sari*, which refers to a distinct, though commonly known, item of clothing in South Asia. In her co-authored translation of Rabindranath Tagore's final poems with Saranindranath Tagore (a descendent of the poet), they chose to keep the word *sari* in its original language not only because it had no equivalent in English, but because it was both recognizeable even as it signaled the foreign cultural context. However, they chose to translate the "ghomtá," the part of the sari that young girls pull over their head like a hood, with extended descriptions in English. That is, they found a middle ground between keeping the recognizably foreign term in its original language while translating terms that were too idiosyncratic for readers in the United States (xviii). We followed suit.

One of the biggest challenges we faced in translating Paredes' verse appeared at the poetry's most basic levels—its structure—which butts up against its content. At the very young age in which Paredes writes this collection, he already is experimenting with ideas and discourses that he explores later in his more famous works. As he himself noted, this was a moment of metamorphosis. But among these precocious instances of early brilliance, Paredes also reveals his immaturity as a writer. In other words, his command of the language at this stage in his writing career is sometimes lacking. His poetry reveals major conflicts in three major areas: grammar, rhythm, and rhyme. Paredes' grammar is influenced by several currents including the Spanish Golden Age poets, as well as the Greek Classics and his regional Mexican-American lingo. This poses obvious problems: all throughout the collection, Paredes attempts to reconcile a high Spanish rhetoric with the more popular Tex-Mex idiom. Given that some poems were composed when Paredes was still in his teens and still forming as a poet and cultural worker, the reconciliation is not always successful. In many occasions, his rhetoric wanders astray from an initial high rhetoric into a convoluted and even pretentious diction, which sometimes is paired with vernacular syntax and idioms. This is not to say that vernacular idioms are not complex enough to carry complex ideas. On the contrary. The dissonance arises because the fusion of vernacular South Texas anti-imperialist and existentialist angst sometimes involves elite tone and word choice. In all fairness to Paredes, it must be noted that this tension almost is unavoidable: it arises as a function of his attempt to explore a unique and challenging array of complex ideas in folk speech and, on the other hand, folk sensibilities in formal poetic diction and syntax. This issue of diction is further complicated by his attempt to mimic the highly formal forms of Spanish and British Renaissance poetry.

Furthermore, even though he claims in his prologue that the majority of the grammatical errors were corrected, Paredes is constantly convoluting his poetry by switching or misspelling tenses. Moreover, for the sake of the aforementioned attempt of a higher order of political and existentialist rhetoric, he leaves out pronouns or articles. This in turn, makes it harder to link a particular description to its origin or identify a metaphor's tenor and vehicle in some poems. A minor though no less significant feature of Paredes' early verse is his irregular use of spacing and indentation. At some points, Paredes does so with no clear logic. For instance, he splits a particular idea in an attempt to force the reader to continue his reading. It is as though he attempts an interstanza enjambment, but instead of increasing the crescendo of the poem, he brakes its rhythm. A similar issue arises from his irregular use of indentation. As with his use of spacing, his indentation practices certainly achieve their caesura goals, but at other times Paredes leads his audience into unnecessary pauses or forced (and false) starts of particular ideas. Capitalization proved to be another constant irregularity in his verse. Throughout the text, it appears as if Paredes abides more to the visual aesthetics of the poem on the page and omits standard capitalization. For the translation, we not only have given the collection a new language, but have attempted to standardize some of these uses based on contemporary publishing conventions.

Another troubling aspect of the collection concerned Paredes' rhyme and rhythm. All throughout the collection, Paredes maintains two rhyme schemes. This includes alternating rhymed lines *abab cdcd* and also the schema of the Italian, or Petrarchan, Sonnet form, which is distinguished by the octave rhyming *abba abba* and the sestet *cdecde*, *cdcdcd*, or *cdedce*. At other instances, Paredes is unable to follow through with these models throughout the entire poem even though this obviously was his intent. That is, it is clear that in some instances he attempts to follow a particular scheme, but midway is unable to find the right word or the rhyme and thus decides to degenerate into free verse. In the translation, however, we have taken the liberty of trying to preserve Paredes' intended rhyme schemes even when he himself fails to do so. In other cases, we break his original rhyme schemes in favor of alliteration when the "sound" works better in English.

As far as his rhythm is concerned, Paredes finds a second voice in music, which enhances his poetic rhythm. The musicality of the collection is arguably one of its chief virtues, but it also presented us with another challenge: whether to maintain his rhyme or aim towards the preservation of rhythm. Since Paredes is continually referring to the "music" in his life—indeed, he was an accomplished pianist and guitarist—it seemed appropriate to approximate the music of each poem by either rhyme, rhythm or both, whatever was required in English. Therefore, at times, the translated rhymes are not as close, but we have tried to combine the best of both worlds by approximating rhymes, using alliteration and maintaining the poetry's original musical tone and rhythm. Overall, Paredes' grammar, rhythm and rhyme, illustrate his incredible talent and maturity for a teenager, but they also reveal the early stage of a writer trying to polish his creative writing skills, which a mature writer attends to through a constant revision process.

Paredes' poetry also reflects musical rhythms, sounds and behavior. For example, the section entitled "La música" presents an array of song-like structures. The section acts as a musical survey containing a *corrido*, a ballad and even a *rumba*. Moreover, Paredes, who was an accomplished musicologist and anthropologist and also a trained folklorist and classicist as well as a renowned guitar and piano virtuoso, permeates his poetry with Neo-classical images, structures and allusions. For instance, in the aforementioned poem, "Fábula," the presence of a tight meter and rhyme along the Classical images of satyrs and fauns displays a broad range of interests and influences. Throughout the collection, Paredes maintains a particular tempo with his rhymes and rhythms. Therefore, when confronted with the structure and patterns of a song such as his "Rima" poems, we chose the compactness and precision of words even if this sometimes required the use of broad analogies. In these music poems, it ultimately was impossible to achieve a literal translation since there were no equivalent words in English. As Rabassa notes, no single word can exist in two languages. Even cognates denote and connote different meanings. They are mere synonyms and each are independent entities. In many cases—especially the song titles—we followed Barker and Tagore's two-pronged compromise.

Our very act of translating Paredes also involved an examination of Paredes' own translations of Donne and Lord Tennyson as well as his translations of *décimas*. As we analyzed Paredes' Spanish translations of Donne's "Song to Celia" and Tennyson's "Crossing the Bar," it became clear that he begins his process with a literal approach, but as the artistry and poetics proceed, Paredes turns to a more figural approach. He never loses track of its origin even as he cannot always rely on synonyms. As such, Paredes provides us with a model of how he himself viewed the art and craft of translating, which we have sought to emulate. His own translation of "Río Bravo" collected in *Between Two Worlds* re-enforced this idea and allowed us to combine the best of both schools of translation theory and practice.

Following Paredes's own model, we took liberties with tense, syntax, and vocabulary, and only explain the more significant changes in footnotes to provide our rationale and to allow the reader to consider the many alternate options that are always available in poetry translations. As noted above, our more controversial translation choices oftentimes are done to preserve the rhyme scheme that Paredes obviously intended to be the central formal feature of the poem. At other times, the changes were undertaken to emphasize the tone or central theme of the composition.

Finally, we must note that in the process of translating *Cantos de adolescencia*, we have come to appreciate it as a remarkable feat of poetry for a teenager and young adult. Indeed, Paredes' inaugural collection of poetry not only pressages Paredes' later greatness, but it heralds it with clever rhymes, sharp accomplished tempos, and lucid expressions of pathos. With full respect and admiration of the original author, we hope to have produced an accurate and pleasing transportation of *Cantos de adolescencia* into English. Any failures in this endeavor are ours; all successes belong to Américo Paredes Manzano.

B.V. Olguín
Omar Vásquez Barbosa
San Antonio & Barcelona
2005

Notes

[1]We use "Mexican American" as a descriptive term to refer to the population of Mexican descent living in the United States from the end of the U.S.-Mexico War in 1848 to the 1960s. The terms "Chicana" and "Chicano," or "Chicana/o," which deliberately invoke an anticolonialist indigenous genealogy for Mexican Americans, refer to the post-1960s Mexican-American population. Our references to Mexican-American and Chicana/o literature correspond to these distinctions.

[2]Paredes was drafted into the U.S. Army in 1944 and served until 1946. He was assigned to work as a political reporter for the U.S. Army Newspaper *Stars and Stripes*, and subsequently covered the war crimes tribunals in Japan.

[3]For studies of Paredes' contribution to Chicana/o cultural studies, see José Limón (1992, 1994); Ramón Saldívar (1990, 2006); José David Saldívar

(1997, 2000); Sonia Saldívar-Hull (2000), Leticia Garza-Falcón (1998); Louis Mendoza (2001); and Olguín (2005).

[4]For studies of Paredes' poetry, see Ramón Saldívar (1993, 1995); José David Saldívar (1997); Limón (1992); Rafael Pérez-Torres (1995). In addition, Ramón Saldívar devotes an entire chapter on Paredes' poetry in his intellectual biography of Paredes that was published after this translation went to press (2006).

[5]For a discussion of Paredes' hybrid poetics, see José David Saldívar (1997) and also Pérez-Torres (1995). For a discussion of the complex spatial ontology of Paredes' short stories characters, see Ramón Saldívar (1994).

[6]The poem "*Alma pocha*" originally was written in 1936 as a sonnet titled "*El pocho*." According to Paredes, it was composed as a response to a call by Texas government officials to commemorate the Texas Centennial Celebration. However, *La Prensa* (San Antonio), which had published several of his poems, declined to publish it due to its satirical tone and materialist critique of the dispossession of the Mexican-American population. The poem ultimately was published by Chicano poet Alurista and the co-editors of the anthology *Flor y Canto II: An Anthology of Chicano Poetry* (1975), and later reprinted in the journal *Maize* (1977). The expanded version, "*Alma pocha*," is included in *Between Two Worlds*. For further discussion of the genealogy of this poem, see *Between Two Worlds*, footnote 4; and also Paredes' preface to his aborted collection *Various Verse*, which he titles "To the Small Group of Compañeros for Whom this Collection is Intended," in the Américo Paredes Papers, Box 17, Folder 5. The two versions of this poem are included in the Addenda.

[7]Paredes' historical novel *George Washington Gómez* was begun in 1936 and completed in 1940. It was not published until 1990 by Arte Público Press.

[8]See typed log entry for Monday, April 16, 1979. Américo Paredes Papers, Box 7, Folder 19.

[9]Ibid. In the Introduction to *Between Two Worlds* Paredes discusses the destruction of some of his poetry. Nicolás Kanellos verifies this incident as do the Américo Paredes Papers, which include sample tables of contents listing poems that are now lost.

[10]This is the verbatim goal that prefaces all project publications. For an overview of the *Recovering the U.S. Hispanic Literary Heritage Project*, see Kanellos (1993) and also Ramón A. Gutiérrez and Génaro Padilla (1993).

[11]Some contemporary Chicana/o oral bards are San Antonio-based Angela De Hoyos and Nephtali De León, both of whom are renowned for their ability to spontaneously produce declamatory poems for a variety of occasions.

[12]"*El México-Texano*," *La Voz* (Brownsville, Texas), August 31, 1941. Américo Paredes Papers, Box 12, Folder 1. In the footnote to the version reprinted in *Between Two Worlds*, Paredes provides a historiography of the poem:

> Perhaps the best known of my efforts at versifying. The first version was done in Spring 1934, when I was a senior in high school. Composed while walking the 21 blocks home from school one afternoon and written down—with revisions—shortly afterward. This second, written version became current in manuscript form in south Texas, was used in political campaigns, was reprinted a few times as anonymous, and entered oral tradition locally. Collected in Brownsville as "folk poetry" in the 1960s by a student of one of my colleagues, Roger D. Abrahams. When it began to circulate in manuscript, writer Hart Stilwell criticized the language as sounding too much like the state "Italian" dialect of the time. I made revisions and it is this third version, done in 1935, that appears here. (139)

[13]"The Mexico-Texan," periodical unknown. Américo Paredes Papers, Box 12, Folder 1.

[14]"The Mexico-Texan," *Brownsville Herald*, circa 1936. Américo Paredes Papers, Box 12, Folder 1.

[15]The other two known copies of *Cantos de adolescencia* are housed in the American History Library at UT Austin. All three copies are slightly damaged, with one missing a frontispiece photo of Paredes.

[16]In a letter to Arte Público Press Director Nicolás Kanellos dated June 23, 1989, Paredes asks Kanellos to remove the poem at the urging of his wife. She was uncomfortable with the morbid farewell tone of the poem, in which Paredes asks to be cremated. Américo Paredes Papers, Box 18, Folder 3.

[17]Ibid.

[18]The Américo Paredes Papers contain poems from many of these figures. Paredes also identifies the writing circle members in a letter to Manuel Cruz, a newcomer to the group, dated January 7, 1943. Américo Paredes Papers, Box 5, Folder 6. Elsewhere, Paredes recalls that his then-student José Limón borrowed some of these primary materials for a planned study on this network of South Texas writers, which was never completed.

[19]We briefly discuss the *décima* form in the annotations in the collection. For a more thorough treatment of this Mexican folk form, see Paredes and Foss (1968).

[20]See untitled English-language log in the Américo Paredes Papers, Box 7, Folder 19.

[21]Ibid.

[22]For a general discussion of Chicana/o cultural nationalist poetry, see Pérez-Torres (1995) and Cordelia Chávez Candelaria (1986).

[23]For an introductory periodization of Mexican-American literature, see Raymond Paredes (1993). For an incisive critique of the generational paradigm, see Mendoza (2001).

[24]Paredes's draft of a short story "River Man," which was never published, originally was outlined on U.S. Army stationary. This story idea includes a sketch of the terrain map for the setting drawn on paper stamped "Armed Forces Information Division, Information & Education Detachment." See Américo Paredes Papers, Box 12, Folder 2.

[25]This log is located in the Américo Paredes Papers, Box 7, Folder 19. For a discussion of African American "signifying," see Gates (1987). For a discussion of the related Latin American and U.S. Latina/o permutations known as *cábula* and *choteo*, see José David Saldívar (2000).

[26]According to Paredes, the drawing was done by Salomé McAllen Scanlan, whom Paredes identifies as a teacher and good family friend who also was his supervisor when he was a student assistant in junior college.

[27]See log, Américo Paredes Papers, Box 7, Folder 19.

[28]See log, Américo Paredes Papers, Box 7, Folder 18. Some song lyrics and musical scores are included in Paredes' improvised songbooks and some are loose.

[29]See log, Américo Paredes Papers, Box 7, Folder 19.

[30]See extended correspondence between Hinojosa, Paredes, and Kanellos, Américo Paredes Papers, Box 18, Folder 3.

[31]Cited in Bassnett 1996, p.70.

Works Cited

Arnold C. Vento, Alurista, and José Flores Peregrino, eds. *Flor y Canto II: An Anthology of Chicano Poetry.* Austin: Pajarito Publications, 1975.

Anzaldúa, Gloria. *Borderlands/La Frontera: The New Mestiza*. San Francisco: Spinsters/Aunt Lute, 1987.

Arteaga, Alfred. "An Other Tongue." *An Other Tongue: Nation and Ethnicity in the Linguistic Borderlands*. Ed. Alfred Arteaga. Durham: Duke UP, 1994. 9-33.

Barker, Wendy. "Preface." *Rabindranath Tagore: Final Poems*. Trans. Wendy Barker and Saranindranath Tagore, New York: George Brazillier, 2001. xi-xxvii.

Bassnett, Susan. *Translation Studies. Revised Edition*. New York: Routledge, 1996.

Bhabha, Homi K. "Of Mimicry and Men: The Ambivalence of Colonial Discourse." *October* 28 (1984): 125-33.

Calderón, Héctor and José Rósbel López-Morín. "Interview with Américo Paredes." *Nepantla: Views from South* 1:1 (2000): 197-228.

Candelaria, Cordelia. *Chicano Poetry: A Critical Introduction*. Wesport: Greenwood P, 1986.

Chabram-Dernersesian, Angie. "I Throw Punches for My Race, But I Don't Want to Be a Man: Writing Us—Chica-nos (Girl, Us) / Chicanas—into the Movement Script." *Cultural Studies*. Eds. Lawrence Grossberg, Cary Nelson, and Paula A. Treichler. New York: Routledge, 1992. 81-95.

De Hoyos, Angela. *Chicano Poems for the Barrio*. Bloomington: Backstage Books, 1975.

———. *Arise, Chicano, and Other Poems*. San Antonio: M&A Editions, 1975.

De León, Nephtalí. *Chicanos: Our Background and Out Pride*. Lubbock: Trucha Publications, 1972.

Gates, Henry Louis. *The Signifying Monkey: A Theory of Afro-American Literary Criticism*. New York: Oxford UP, 1987.

Gutiérrez, Ramón, and Genaro Padilla. "Introduction." *Recovering the U.S. Hispanic Literary Heritage*. Eds. Ramón Gutiérrez and Genaro Padilla. Houston: Arte Público Press, 1993. 17-25.

Herrera-Sobek, Maria. "Nation, Nationality, and Nationalism: Américo Paredes' Paradigms of Self and Country." Conference Presentation, *Pasó Por Aquí: An Américo Paredes Symposium*, University of Texas at Austin, May 3, 2001.

Kanellos, Nicolás. "Foreword." Gutiérrez and Padilla 13-5.

Limón, José E. *American Encounters: Greater Mexico, The United States, and the Erotics of Culture*. Boston: Beacon Press, 1998.

———. "Américo Paredes: A Man from the Border." *Revista Chicano-Riqueña* 8:3 (Summer 1980): 1-5.

———. *Dancing with the Devil: Society and Cultural Poetics in Mexican American South Texas*. Madison: U of Wisconsin P, 1994.

———. *Mexican Ballads, Chicano Poems: History and Influence in Mexican-American Social Poetry*. Berkeley: U of California P, 1992.

Medrano, Manuel, Dir. *Américo Paredes: Pasó Por Aquí*. Prod. U of Texas at Brownsville, 2001.

Mendoza, Louis Gerard. *Historia: The Literary Making of Chicana and Chicano History*. College Station: Texas A&M P, 2001.

Olguín, B.V. "Reassessing Pocho Poetics: Américo Paredes' Poetry and the (Trans)National Question." *Aztlán* 30:1 (Spring 2004): 87-121.

Paredes, Américo. *Cantos de adolescencia*. San Antonio: Librería Española, 1937.

————. *Folklore and Culture on the Texas-Mexico Border*. Austin: U Texas P, 1993.

————. *The Hammon and the Beans and Other Stories*. Houston: Arte Público Press, 1994.

————. "Ichiro Kikuchi." *The Hammon and the Beans, And Other Stories*. Houston: Arte Público Press, 1994. 151-9.

————. Letter to Alurista. October 19, 1974. Nettie Benson Latin American Library Special Collections. Américo Paredes Papers. Box 57, Folder 7.

————. Letter to Rolando Hinojosa. May 30, 1980. Nettie Benson Latin American Library Special Collections. Américo Paredes Papers. Box 64, Folder 2.

————. "El Pocho." Nettie Benson Latin American Library Special Collections. Américo Paredes Papers. Box 57, Folder 7.

————. "Prologue." *Between Two Worlds*. Houston: Arte Público Press, 1991. 9-11.

————. *A Texas-Mexican Cancionero: Folksongs of the Lower Border*. Austin: U Texas P, 1995.

————. *With His Pistol in His Hand: A Border Ballad and Its Hero*. Austin: University of Texas Press, 1958.

————, and George Foss. *The Décima on the Texas-Mexican Border*. Austin: Institute of Latin American Studies Offprint Series, 1968.

Paredes, Raymund. "Mexican-American Literature: An Overview." Gutiérrez and Padilla 31-51.

Paz, Octavio. *The Labyrinth of Solitude: Life and Thought in Mexico*. Trans. Lysander Kemp. New York: Grove Press, 1961.

Pérez-Torres, Rafael. *Movements in Chicano Poetry: Against Myths, Against Margins*. Cambridge: Cambridge UP, 1995.

Rabassa, Gregory. "No Two Snowflakes Are Alike: Translation as Metaphor." *The Craft of Translation*. Eds. John Biguenet and Rainer Schulte. Chicago: U of Chicago P, 1989. 1-12.

Saldívar, José David. *Border Matters: Remapping American Cultural Studies*. Berkeley: U of California P, 1997.

————. *The Dialectics of Our America: Genealogy, Cultural Critique, and Literary History*. Durham: Duke UP, 1991.

————. "The Location of Américo Paredes's Border Thinking." *Nepantla: Views from the South* 1:1 (2000): 191-95.

————. "Looking Awry at 1898: Roosevelt, Montejo, Paredes, and Mariscal." *American Literary History* 12:3 (2000): 387-406.

Saldívar, Ramón. "Américo Paredes." *Updating the Literary West*. Ed. Thomas J. Lyon. Fort Worth: Texas Christian UP, 1997. 633-37.

————. "Américo Paredes and the Transnational Imaginary." *Brackenridge Distinguished Lecture*, University of Texas at San Antonio, February 22, 2001.

————. "Bordering on Modernity: Américo Paredes' Between Two Worlds and the Imagining of Utopian Social Space." *Stanford Humanities Review* 3:1 (Winter 1993): 54-66.

————. "The Borders of Modernity: Américo Paredes's Between Two Worlds and the Chicano National Subject." Ed. David Palumbo-Liu. *The Ethnic Canon: Histories, Institutions, and Interventions*. Minneapolis: U of Minnesota P, 1995. 71-87.

————. *The Borderlands of Culture: Américo Paredes and the Transnational Imaginary*. Durham: Duke UP, 2006.

————. *Chicano Narrative: The Dialectics of Difference*. Madison: Wisconsin U of Wisconsin P, 1990.

————. "Introduction." *The Hammon and the Beans and Other Stories*. Américo Paredes. Houston: Arte Público Press, 1994. vii-li.

Saldívar-Hull, Sonia. *Feminism on the Border: Chicana Gender Politics and Literature.* U of California P, 2000.

Suarez, Mario. "Kid Zopilote." *Arizona Quarterl*y 3 (Summer 1947): 112-37.

Venegas, Daniel. *The Adventures of Don Chipote, or, When Parrots Breast-Feed.* Trans. Ethriam Cash Brammer. Houston: Arte Público Press, 2000.

Ybarra-Frausto, Tomás. "The Chicano Movement and the Emergence of Chicano Poetic Consciousness." *New Directions in Chicano Scholarship*. Eds. Ricardo Romo and Raymund Paredes. La Jolla: University of California at San Diego, Chicano Studies Program, 1978. 81-110.

The Ballad of Gregorio Cortez. Metro Goldwyn Mayer, 1984.

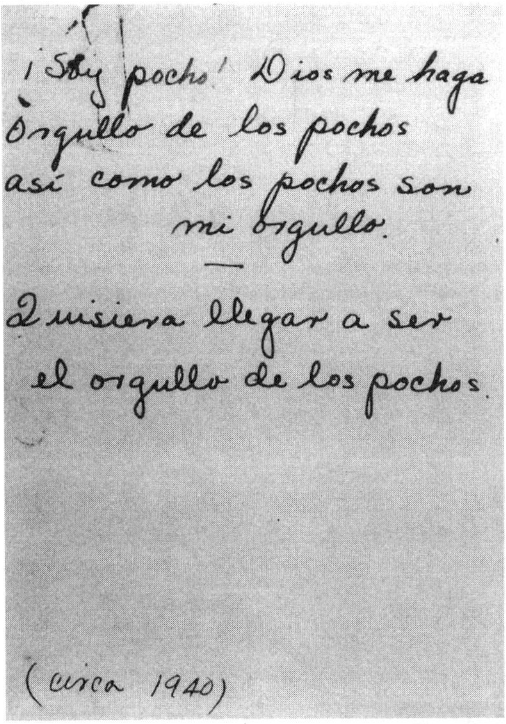
¡Soy pocho! Dios me haga
orgullo de los pochos
así como los pochos son
mi orgullo.
—
Quisiera llegar a ser
el orgullo de los pochos.
(circa 1940)

Figure 1. Handwritten limerick by Paredes, circa 1940. Américo Paredes Papers, Box 7, Folder 19. Courtesy of the Nettie Lee Benson Latin American Collection, University of Texas Libraries, The University of Texas at Austin.

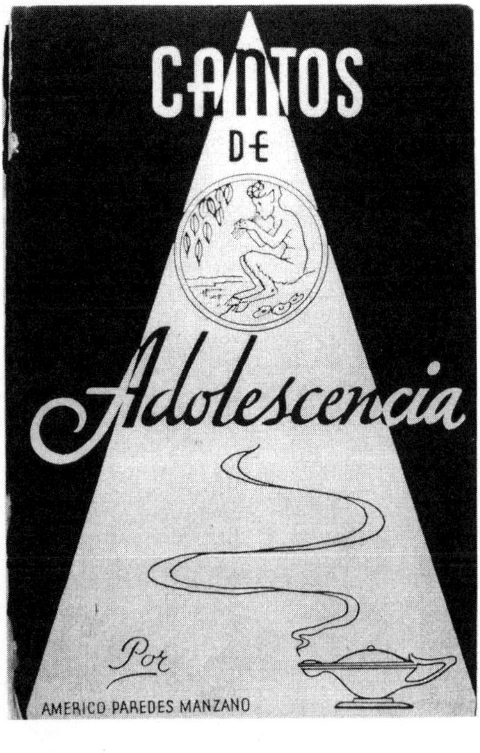

Figure 2. Cover to original edition of *Cantos de adolescencia* (San Antonio, 1937). Américo Paredes Papers, Box 11, Folder 4.

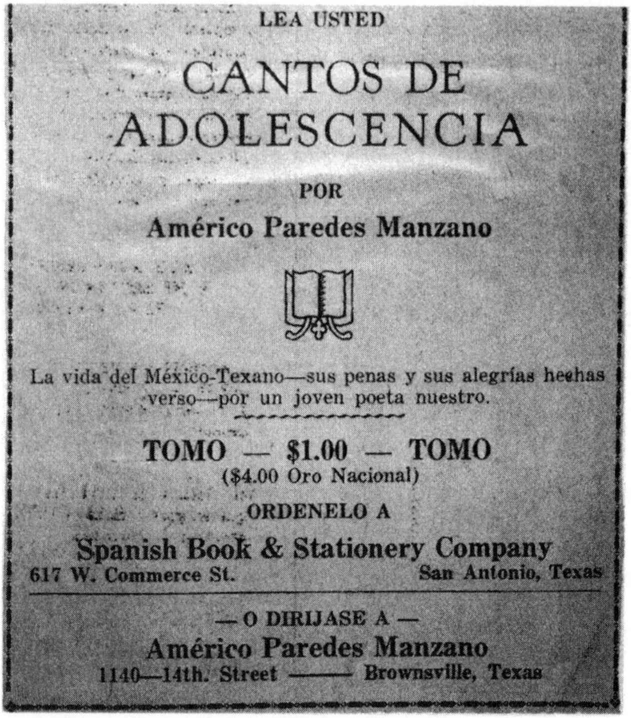

Figure 3. Original advertisement for *Cantos de adolescencia*, periodical and date unknown. Américo Paredes Papers, Box 12, Folder 1.

Figure 4. Announcement for poetry reading by Américo Paredes Manzano. *Brownsville Herald*, circa 1930s. Américo Paredes Papers, Box 12, Folder 1.

GRISHAM'S JINGLE CONTEST

Here is the winner for today:

Great oaks from little acorns grow—
Or so the poets sing.
To make you grow like oaks and such
Good Grisham's milk's the thing.

Americo Paredes, 1140 14th Street

If the writer of this jingle will call at the Grisham's Ice Cream company, a pint of Grisham's Angel Food Ice Cream will be given free.

GRISHAM ICE CREAM CO.

440 W. Elizabeth

Phone 152 Brownsville

Figure 5. Award announcement, periodical unknown, circa 1930s. Américo Paredes Papers, Box 12, Folder 1.

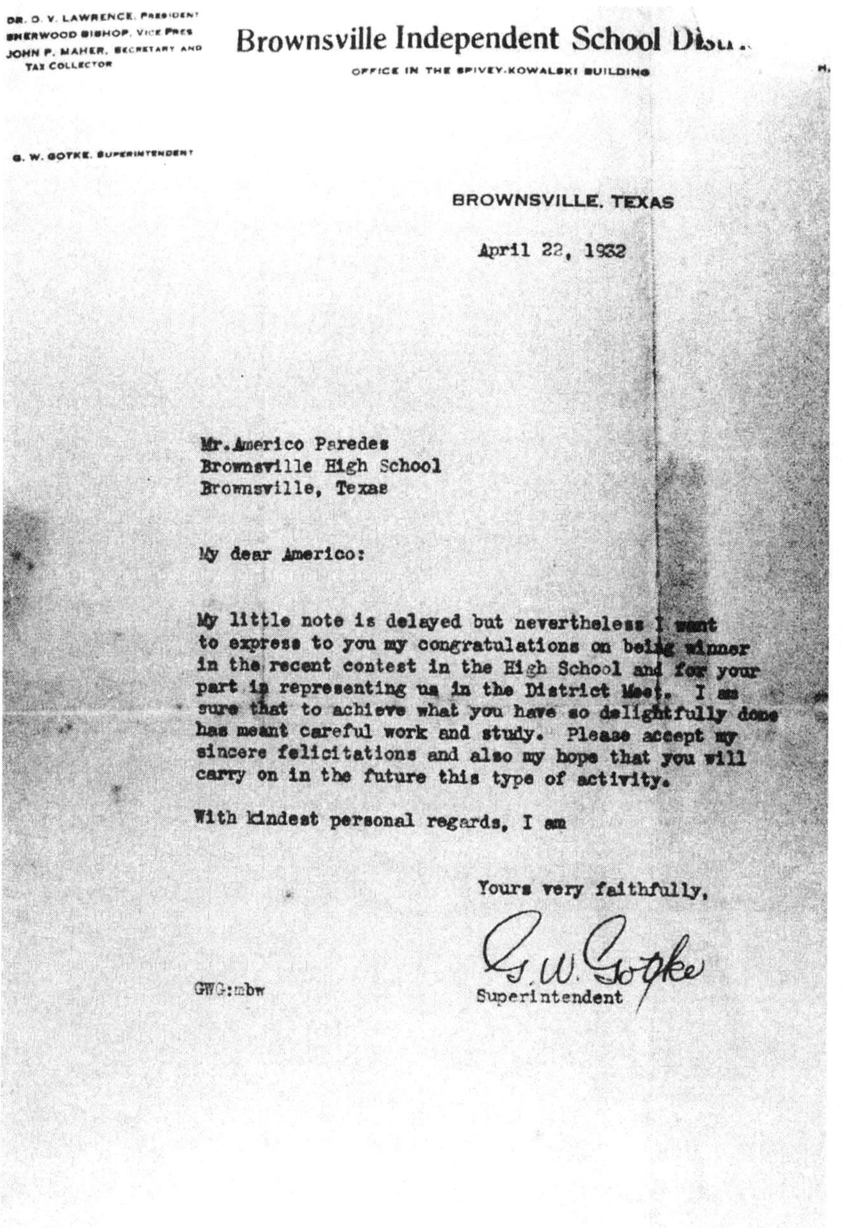

DR. O. V. LAWRENCE, PRESIDENT
SHERWOOD BISHOP, VICE PRES
JOHN P. MAHER, SECRETARY AND TAX COLLECTOR

G. W. GOTKE, SUPERINTENDENT

Brownsville Independent School Dist...

OFFICE IN THE SPIVEY-KOWALSKI BUILDING

BROWNSVILLE, TEXAS

April 22, 1932

Mr. Americo Paredes
Brownsville High School
Brownsville, Texas

My dear Americo:

My little note is delayed but nevertheless I want to express to you my congratulations on being winner in the recent contest in the High School and for your part in representing us in the District Meet. I am sure that to achieve what you have so delightfully done has meant careful work and study. Please accept my sincere felicitations and also my hope that you will carry on in the future this type of activity.

With kindest personal regards, I am

Yours very faithfully,

G. W. Gotke
Superintendent

GWG:mbw

Figure 6. Correspondence from G.W. Gotke, Superintendent, Brownsville Independent School District, April 22, 1932. Américo Paredes Papers, Box 6, Folder 1.

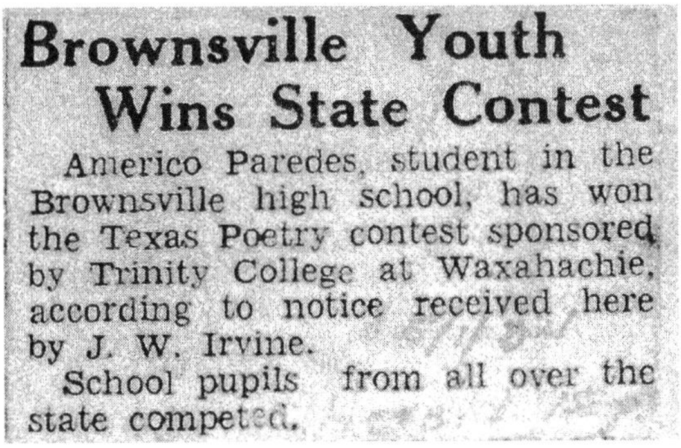

Brownsville Youth Wins State Contest

Americo Paredes, student in the Brownsville high school, has won the Texas Poetry contest sponsored by Trinity College at Waxahachie, according to notice received here by J. W. Irvine.

School pupils from all over the state competed.

Figure 7. Award announcement, *Brownsville Herald*, May 1, 1934. Américo Paredes Papers, Box 12, Folder 1.

UN JOVEN MEXICANO GANO UN CONCURSO DE POESIA DEL ESTADO DE TEXAS

SERVICIO ESPECIAL

Brownsville, Texas, abril 27.—El joven mexicano Américo Paredes, estudiante del último año de la escuela Superior de Brownsville, ha recibido noticias de que su Soneto, "Night" (La Noche) obtuvo el primer premio en un concurso de poesía en el Estado de Texas, que patrocinó la Universidad de Trinity, de Waxachie, Texas.

El segundo y tercer premio les fueron concedidos a estudiantes de Dallas y de Paris, Texas.

En el Concurso tomaron parte los estudiantes de todas las escuelas superiores del Estado, habiéndose sometido a los jueces centenares de poesías.

La Srita. Catharine Donnell, secretaria del "Scriptcrafters" Club de la Universidad de Trinity, notificó al joven Paredes el honor que le había sido concedido.

Elogiosos comentarios y calurosas felicitaciones de parte de sus condiscípulos ha recibido el joven Paredes, pues es verdaderamente honroso que un joven mexicano haya triunfado en un concurso tan difícil y en un idioma extranjero.

Paredes cuenta 18 años de edad, y es hijo del señor Justo Paredes y de la señora Cleotilde Manzano de Paredes, con residencia en la calle 14 entre las de Jackson y Van Buren.

Figure 8. Award announcement, *La Prensa de San Antonio*, April 29, 1934. Américo Paredes Papers, Box 12, Folder 1.

Brownsville Boy Wins In State Poetry Contest

BROWNSVILLE, May 2.—(Sp) — "Night", written by Americo Paredes, 18-year old senior high school student, Brownsville, won first prize in the state-wide contest sponsored by Trinity University, it was announced here today in a letter from Miss Catherine Donnell, secretary of the Scriptcraft club, Waxahachie, Texas.

The poem is as follow:

"Exotic beauty! Dusky Moorish queen!
Dark Night, you are the fairest thing of all,
For when you let your sable mantle fall
Upon the day's hot, weary, shifting scene,
The rest, with smiling face and look serene,
And soothing sleep come softly at your call.
They bring relief to troubles that like gall
Through all the day molesting us have been.
But when, o'er hill and plain, through court and hall
You stalk, be-perfumed and in robes of dew,
And when you speak, majestic, black, and tall,
In voiceless haunting tones, the bards are few
Whose souls your splendor does not hold in thrall
So that they strike the lyre and sing to you!"

Figure 9. Award announcement, *Valley Morning Star*, May 3, 1934. Américo Paredes Papers, Box 12, Folder 1.

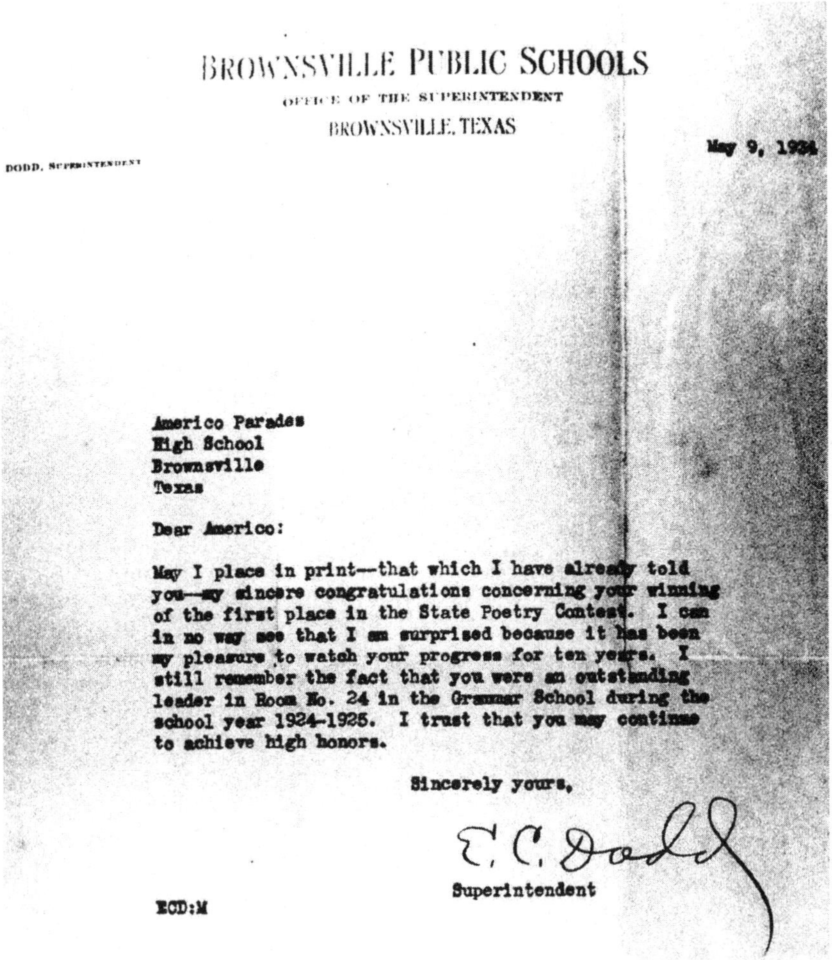

BROWNSVILLE PUBLIC SCHOOLS
OFFICE OF THE SUPERINTENDENT
BROWNSVILLE, TEXAS

DODD, SUPERINTENDENT

May 9, 1934

Americo Parades
High School
Brownsville
Texas

Dear Americo:

May I place in print—that which I have already told you—my sincere congratulations concerning your winning of the first place in the State Poetry Contest. I can in no way see that I am surprised because it has been my pleasure to watch your progress for ten years. I still remember the fact that you were an outstanding leader in Room No. 24 in the Grammar School during the school year 1924-1925. I trust that you may continue to achieve high honors.

Sincerely yours,

E. C. Dodd

Superintendent

ECD:M

Figure 10. Correspondence from E.D. Dodd, Superintendent, Brownsville Public Schools, May 9, 1934. Américo Paredes Papers, Box 6, Folder 1.

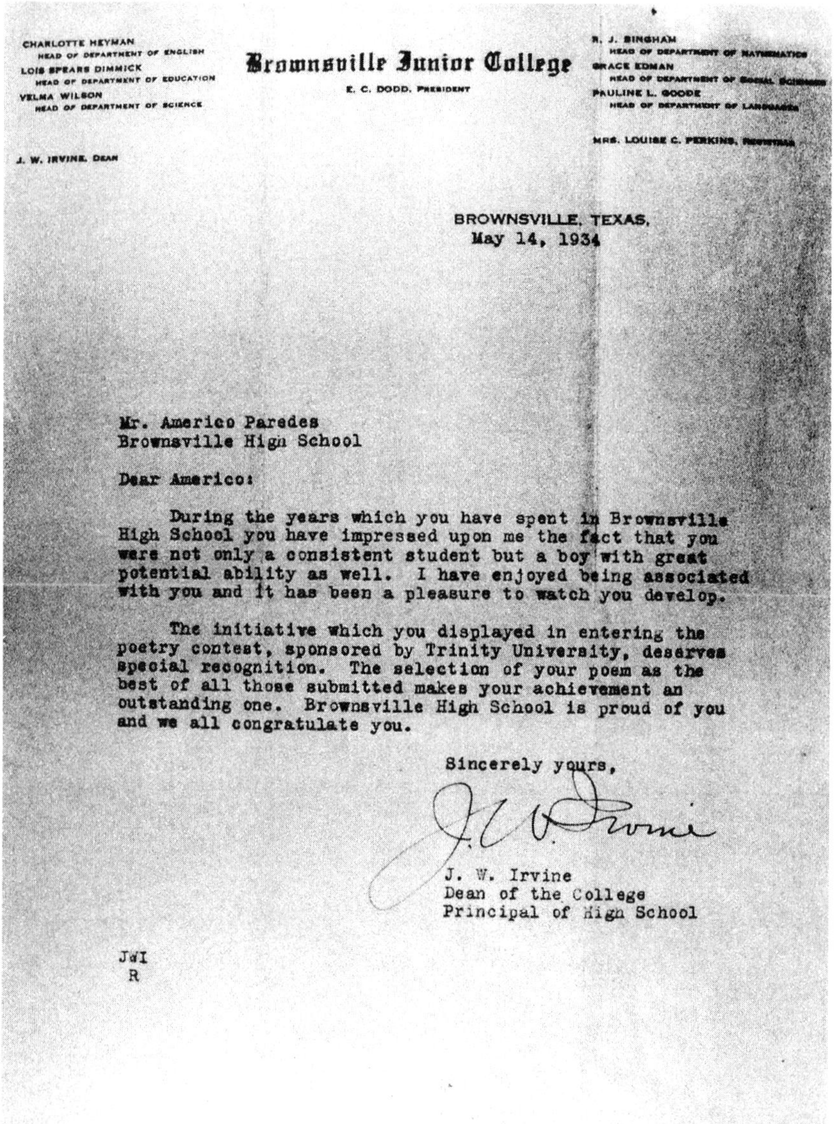

CHARLOTTE HEYMAN
HEAD OF DEPARTMENT OF ENGLISH
LOIS SPEARS DIMMICK
HEAD OF DEPARTMENT OF EDUCATION
VELMA WILSON
HEAD OF DEPARTMENT OF SCIENCE

J. W. IRVINE, DEAN

Brownsville Junior College

E. C. DODD, PRESIDENT

R. J. BINGHAM
HEAD OF DEPARTMENT OF MATHEMATICS
GRACE EDMAN
HEAD OF DEPARTMENT OF SOCIAL SCIENCES
PAULINE L. GOODE
HEAD OF DEPARTMENT OF LANGUAGES

MRS. LOUISE C. PERKINS, REGISTRAR

BROWNSVILLE, TEXAS,
May 14, 1934

Mr. Americo Paredes
Brownsville High School

Dear Americo:

During the years which you have spent in Brownsville High School you have impressed upon me the fact that you were not only a consistent student but a boy with great potential ability as well. I have enjoyed being associated with you and it has been a pleasure to watch you develop.

The initiative which you displayed in entering the poetry contest, sponsored by Trinity University, deserves special recognition. The selection of your poem as the best of all those submitted makes your achievement an outstanding one. Brownsville High School is proud of you and we all congratulate you.

Sincerely yours,

J. W. Irvine

J. W. Irvine
Dean of the College
Principal of High School

JWI
R

Figure 11. Correspondence from J.W. Irvine, Dean, Brownsville Junior College, May 14, 1934. Américo Paredes Papers, Box 6, Folder 1.

106 Lee Penn Street
Waxahachie, Texas
April 30, 1934

Dear Mr. Paredes,

I am very glad to inform you on behalf of the Scriptcrafters' Club of Trinity University that your poem, "Night", won first place in the high school division of the Annual Poetry Meet.

You will receive, in a few days, a prize with our congratulations.

Wishing you much future success with your poetry, I am,

Sincerely,

Catharine Donnell,
Sec.-Treas. Scriptcrafters' Club
Trinity University

Figure 12. Correspondence from Catharine Donnel, Secretary, Scriptcrafter's Club, Trinity University, April 30, 1934. Américo Paredes Papers, Box 18, Folder 8.

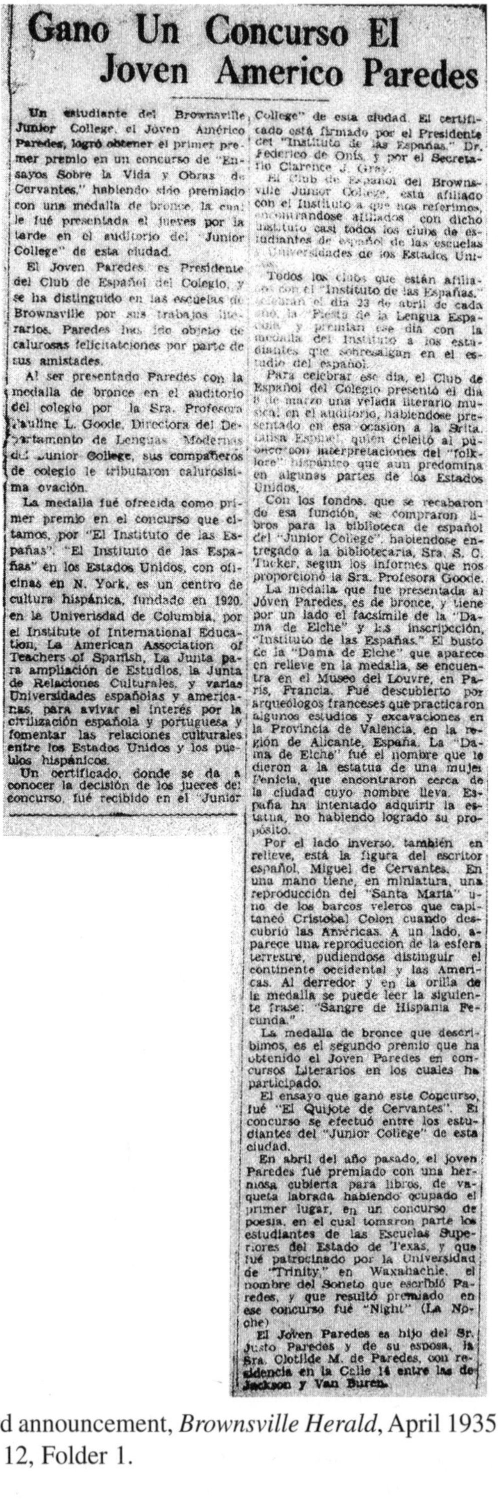

Gano Un Concurso El Joven Americo Paredes

Un estudiante del Brownsville Junior College, el Jóven Américo Paredes, logró obtener el primer premio en un concurso de "Ensayos Sobre la Vida y Obras de Cervantes," habiendo sido premiado con una medalla de bronce, la cual le fué presentada el jueves por la tarde en el auditorio del "Junior College" de esta ciudad.

El Joven Paredes es Presidente del Club de Español del Colegio, y se ha distinguido en las escuelas de Brownsville por sus trabajos literarios. Paredes has ido objeto de calurosas felicitaciones por parte de sus amistades.

Al ser presentado Paredes con la medalla de bronce en el auditorio del colegio por la Sra. Profesora Pauline L. Goode, Directora del Departamento de Lenguas Modernas del Junior College, sus compañeros de colegio le tributaron calurosísima ovación.

La medalla fué ofrecida como primer premio en el concurso que citamos, por "El Instituto de las Españas". "El Instituto de las Españas" en los Estados Unidos, con oficinas en N. York, es un centro de cultura hispánica, fundado en 1920, en la Univerisdad de Columbia, por el Institute of International Education, La American Association of Teachers of Spanish, La Junta para ampliación de Estudios, la Junta de Relaciones Culturales, y varias Universidades españolas y americanas, para avivar el interés por la civilización española y portuguesa y fomentar las relaciones culturales entre los Estados Unidos y los pueblos hispánicos.

Un certificado, donde se da a conocer la decisión de los jueces del concurso, fué recibido en el "Junior College" de esta ciudad. El certificado está firmado por el Presidente del "Instituto de las Españas," Dr. Federico de Onís, y por el Secretario Clarence J. Gray.

El Club de Español del Brownsville Junior College, está afiliado con el Instituto a que nos referimos, encontrandose afiliados con dicho Instituto casi todos los clubs de estudiantes de español de las escuelas y Universidades de los Estados Unidos.

Todos los clubs que están afiliados con el "Instituto de las Españas," celebran el día 23 de abril de cada año, la "Fiesta de la Lengua Española" y premian ese día con la medalla del Instituto a los estudiantes que sobresalgan en el estudio del español.

Para celebrar ese día, el Club de Español del Colegio presentó el día 8 de marzo una velada literario musical en el auditorio, habiendose presentado en esa ocasion a la Srita. Luisa Espinel, quien deleitó al público con interpretaciones del "folklore" hispánico que aun predomina en algunas partes de los Estados Unidos.

Con los fondos, que se recabaron de esa función, se compraron libros para la biblioteca de español del "Junior College", habiendose entregado a la bibliotecaria, Sra. S. C. Tucker, segun los informes que nos proporcionó la Sra. Profesora Goode.

La medalla que fue presentada al Jóven Paredes, es de bronce, y tiene por un lado el facsímile de la "Dama de Elche" y la inscripcción, "Instituto de las Españas." El busto de la "Dama de Elche" que aparece en relieve en la medalla, se encuentra en el Museo del Louvre, en París, Francia. Fué descubierto por arqueólogos franceses que practicaron algunos estudios y excavaciones en la Provincia de Valencia, en la región de Alicante, España. La "Dama de Elche" fué el nombre que le dieron a la estatua de una mujer Fenicia, que encontraron cerca de la ciudad cuyo nombre lleva. España ha intentado adquirir la estatua, no habiendo logrado su propósito.

Por el lado inverso, también en relieve, está la figura del escritor español, Miguel de Cervantes. En una mano tiene, en miniatura, una reproducción del "Santa María" uno de los barcos veleros que capitaneó Cristobal Colon cuando descubrió las Américas. A un lado, aparece una reproduccion de la esfera terrestre, pudiendose distinguir el continente occidental y las Americas. Al derredor y en la orilla de la medalla se puede leer la siguiente frase: "Sangre de Hispania Fecunda."

La medalla de bronce que describimos, es el segundo premio que ha obtenido el Joven Paredes en concursos Literarios en los cuales ha participado.

El ensayo que ganó este Concurso, fué "El Quijote de Cervantes". El concurso se efectuó entre los estudiantes del "Junior College" de esta ciudad.

En abril del año pasado, el joven Paredes fué premiado con una hermosa cubierta para libros, de vaqueta labrada habiendo ocupado el primer lugar, en un concurso de poesia, en el cual tomaron parte los estudiantes de las Escuelas Superiores del Estado de Texas, y que fué patrocinado por la Universidad de "Trinity," en Waxahachie, el nombre del Soneto que escribió Paredes, y que resultó premiado en ese concurso fué "Night" (La Noche)

El Jóven Paredes es hijo del Sr. Justo Paredes y de su esposa, la Sra. Clotilde M. de Paredes, con residencia en la Calle 14 entre las de Jackson y Van Buren.

Figure 13. Award announcement, *Brownsville Herald*, April 1935. Américo Paredes Papers, Box 12, Folder 1.

BANQUETE EN HONOR DE UN JOVEN BARDO

Se Verifico Ayer En Matamoros en Honor De Americo Paredes Manzano

(Especial Para El Heraldo)

MATAMOROS, Tamps., Sept. 6— El jóven bardo Brownsvillense, Américo Paredes Manzano, fué agasajado por un grupo de prominentes residentes de Matamoros con una comida, en céntrico restaurant de esta ciudad el domingo por la tarde, con motivo de la publicación de la primera obra de verso del jóven poeta, titulada "Cantos de Adolescencia."

Durante la opípara comida los comensales discutieron varios asuntos de interés, charlando sobre temas de literatura.

Después de la comida y antes de abandonar la mesa, el Sr. Pedro Garza Uribe, conocido hombre de negocios de esta ciudad fronteriza hizo uso de la palabra, elogiando la labor del jóven poeta de allende el Bravo, por la publicación de su primera obra.

Acto seguido hicieron uso de la palabra los Sres. Lic. Aurelio de León, Florentino Cuéllar, Gerente de la Cámara de Comercio de Matamoros, Gregorio Garza Flores, redactor de "El Regional"; Antonio Valverde Ruiz, Oscar J. del Castillo, Eliseo Paredes, conocido comerciante de Matamoros y por último el jóven bardo, quien dijo verse honrado por el agasajo de que fué objeto, recitando algunas de sus composiciones.

Todas las personas que hicieron uso de la palabra elogiaron calurosamente la labor del jóven poeta Brownsvillense.

El Sr. Valverde Ruiz recitó varios poesías de Villaespesa y otra de Ricardo de León, recibiendo muchos aplausos.

El agasajo fué organizado por el Sr. Gregorio Garza Flores y otras prominentes personas de Matamoros.

Figure 14. Award announcement, *Brownsville Herald*, September 6, 1937. Américo Paredes Papers, Box 12, Folder 1.

BY HART STILWELL

BROWNSVILLE has a young writer who will some day carve a name for himself, even though he's writing only during his spare time.

He's Americo Paredes, employe of Pan American Airways.

You..g Paredes has also composed a half hundred or so songs, mostly in Spanish.

He will have an article on the ballads of the Texas-Mexican border county in an early issue of Southwest Review, published by Southern Methodist University at Dallas.

Figure 15. Award announcement, periodical unknown, circa late 1930s. Américo Paredes Papers, Box 12, Folder 1.

LA PRENSA • DIARIO POPULAR INDEPENDIENTE • SAN ANTONIO, TEXAS

LITERARIOS DE 'LA PRENSA'

El Diario de un Adolescente

A MEXICO

MEXICO, LA ILUSION DEL CONTINENTE

EL SUEÑO DE BOLIVAR

OJOS VERDES

GUADALUPE LA CHINACA

CANCIONES

PASO DOBLE

EL HURACAN

PRIMAVERA EN LA CIUDAD

A UNA SAJONA

PLUMAS NEGRAS

SI TU SUPIERAS

CANTA

THE MEXICO-TEXAN

Figure 16. Two-page pull-out feature of *Cantos de adolescencia* in *La Prensa de San Antonio*, October 18, 1937. Américo Paredes Papers, Box 12, Folder 1.

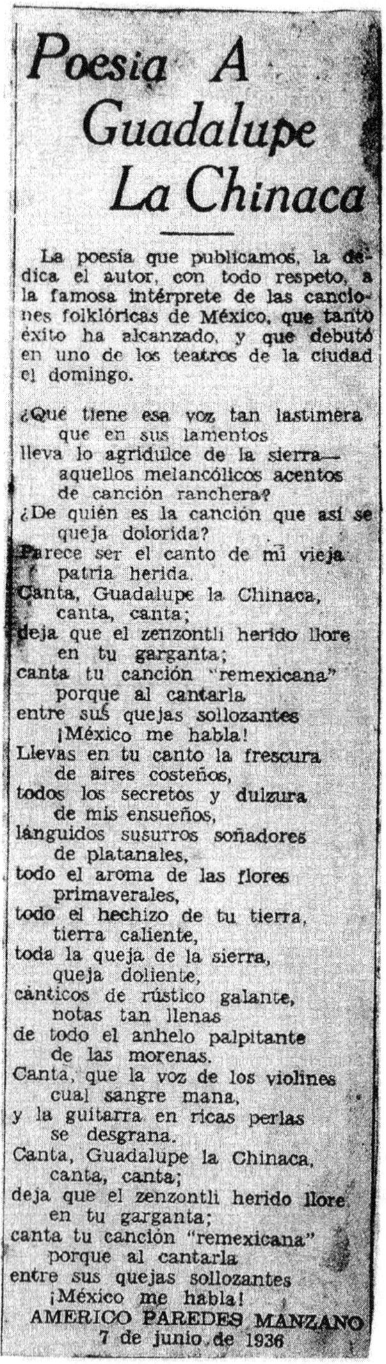

Poesia A Guadalupe La Chinaca

La poesía que publicamos, la dedica el autor, con todo respeto, a la famosa intérprete de las canciones folklóricas de México, que tanto éxito ha alcanzado, y que debutó en uno de los teatros de la ciudad el domingo.

¿Qué tiene esa voz tan lastimera
que en sus lamentos
lleva lo agridulce de la sierra—
aquellos melancólicos acentos
de canción ranchera?
¿De quién es la canción que así se
queja dolorida?
Parece ser el canto de mi vieja
patria herida.
Canta, Guadalupe la Chinaca,
canta, canta;
deja que el zenzontli herido llore
en tu garganta;
canta tu canción "remexicana"
porque al cantarla
entre sus quejas sollozantes
¡México me habla!
Llevas en tu canto la frescura
de aires costeños,
todos los secretos y dulzura
de mis ensueños,
lánguidos susurros soñadores
de platanales,
todo el aroma de las flores
primaverales,
todo el hechizo de tu tierra,
tierra caliente,
toda la queja de la sierra,
queja doliente,
cánticos de rústico galante,
notas tan llenas
de todo el anhelo palpitante
de las morenas.
Canta, que la voz de los violines
cual sangre mana,
y la guitarra en ricas perlas
se desgrana.
Canta, Guadalupe la Chinaca,
canta, canta;
deja que el zenzontli herido llore
en tu garganta;
canta tu canción "remexicana"
porque al cantarla
entre sus quejas sollozantes
¡México me habla!

AMERICO PAREDES MANZANO
7 de junio de 1936

Figure 17. Original version of poem, "Guadalupe la Chinaca." Américo Paredes Papers, Box 12, Folder 1.

Figure 18. Concert poster for performance by "Guadalupe la Chinaca" with verse excerpt from poem of same name, circa 1945. Américo Paredes Papers, Box 12, Folder 1.

Figure 19. Original version of poem, "New Year's Eve," periodical unknown, circa 1930s. Américo Paredes Papers, Box 12, Folder 1.

Domingo 31 de Agosto, 1941 LA VOZ

CHICOTAZOS

EL MEXICO-TEXANO

(Por Américo Paredes Manzano; de Brownsville, Texas, para el Pbro. T. Montero, O. M. I., de San Antonio, Texas).

Para recreo de nuestros lectores, publicamos en esta sección amena de "CHICOTAZOS" la siguiente poesía jocosa, en versos pareados, aunque de rima imperfecta, imitando de lejos el original inglés. Lo hacemos con la venia del autor y con perdón de nuestros lectores méxico-texanos que son sobrado inteligentes para saber dispensar el tono bromista de la composición, cuyo autor es tan méxico-texano y tan buen patriota como el que más.

Nota de LA REDACCION

El méxico-texano, curioso personaje,
Que en la región habita Norte del Río Grande,
De padre mexicano nacido en esta orilla,
No es extraño que a veces la nostalgia le oprima;
En el lenguaje "gringo" él no puede expresarse
Con aquella finura que da la lengua madre;
Ciudadano de Texas le dicen por derecho,
Aunque luego le traten cual si fuera extranjero;
En fin, que por decirlo con muy pocas palabras:
El méxico-texano parece un ser sin patria.

Cuando el Río atraviesa, no le sirve de nada,
Pues el lenguaje fino del otro lado no habla;
Y luego las costumbres por allá son muy otras,
Se extrañan de los nombres, también de las personas;
Desprecian al texano y le dicen por burla:
"Vuélvete con el gringo y que él te preste ayuda....."
En Texas uno es Johnny y allá Don Juan le llaman,
El méxico-texano parece un ser sin patria.

Llegan las elecciones, y el gringo le convida,
Con palabras muy tiernas le declara su estima;
Mezcal y barbacoa completan el milagro
Y brindan como amigos por el triunfo cercano;
Mas termina la fiesta y la amistad se acaba;
El méxico-texano parece un ser sin patria.

Excepto algunos cuantos muy bien considerados,
No cuenta para nada fuera de raros casos;
Dicen que sólo sirve de rémora y de carga
Aunque en paz como en guerra no se libre de taxas;
No tiene voz ni voto, concluida la campaña;
El méxico-texano parece un ser sin patria.

Pero a veces consigue ahogar muy bien sus penas
Y es el día en que logra ingerir una buena......
Pues aunque un ser parezca que no conoce patria,
Tiene sobre los otros esta especial ventaja:
Que puede como uva ponerse celebrando
Las grandes fiestas patrias de uno y otro lado.

Figure 20. Facsimile of Spanish version of "El Mexico-Texano," *La Voz* (Brownsville, Texas), August 31, 1941. Américo Paredes Papers, Box 12, Folder 1.

THE MEXICO-TEXAN

(Esta notable rima es de un autor desconocido que retrata mejor que cien descripciones al méxico-texano. Dicen los LULACS cuando la publicaron por vez primera: "Publicamos esta rima porque contiene más verdad que poesía y todo el que la lea sabrá comprender su mérito.")

The Mexico-Texan, a durn fonny man,
Who lives in the region that's north of the Gran.
Of Mexican father. he born in thees part,
And sometimes he rues it way down in hees heart.
For the Mexico-Texan, he no gotta no lan'
He stomped on da neck on both sides of the Gran.
The dam gringo lingo he no cannot spik,
It twist:. da tong and it maka heem sik.
A cit'zen of Texas they say that he ees...
But then—why they call heem da Mexican Grease?
Soft talk and hard actions he can't understand,
The Mexico-Texan, he no gotta no lan'.
Elections come 'round and the gringos are loud,
They pat on hees back and they maka heem proud.
They give heem mezcal and they heem meet,
They tell heem, "Amigo we can't be defeat"
But after election, he no gotta no fran
The Mexico-Texan, he no gotta no lan'.
Except for a few that in cunning are deft,
He counta so much as an "O" to the left.
He no gotta no voice, all he gotta is da hand,
To work like da burro—he no gotta no lan'
Only one way can hees sorrows all drown,
He'll get drunk as hell when next payday comes 'roun.
For he has one advantage of all other men,
Though the Mexico-Texan he no gotta no lan'
He can gotta so drunk that he thinks he can fly,
Both September da Sixteen and Fourth of July.

Figure 21. Facsimile of reprint of poem, "The Mexico-Texan," periodical and date unknown. Américo Paredes Papers, Box 12, Folder 1.

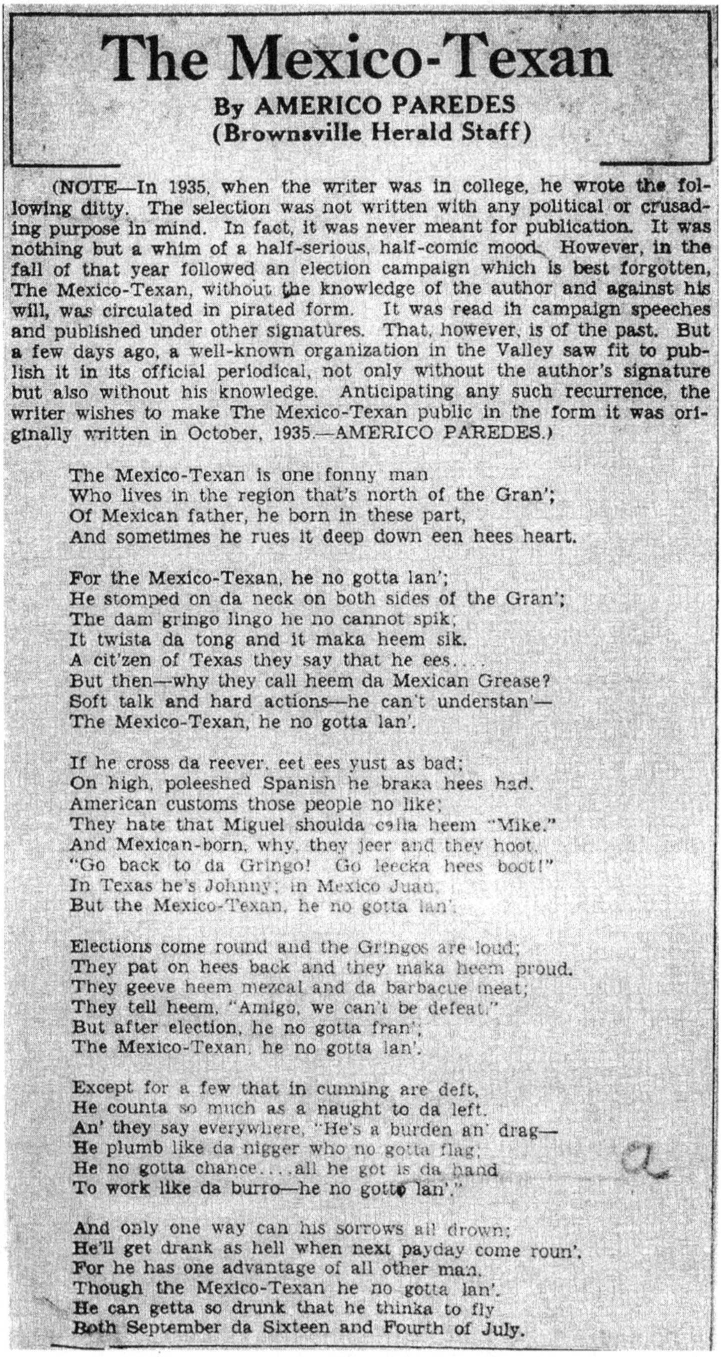

The Mexico-Texan

By AMERICO PAREDES
(Brownsville Herald Staff)

(NOTE—In 1935, when the writer was in college, he wrote the following ditty. The selection was not written with any political or crusading purpose in mind. In fact, it was never meant for publication. It was nothing but a whim of a half-serious, half-comic mood. However, in the fall of that year followed an election campaign which is best forgotten, The Mexico-Texan, without the knowledge of the author and against his will, was circulated in pirated form. It was read in campaign speeches and published under other signatures. That, however, is of the past. But a few days ago, a well-known organization in the Valley saw fit to publish it in its official periodical, not only without the author's signature but also without his knowledge. Anticipating any such recurrence, the writer wishes to make The Mexico-Texan public in the form it was originally written in October, 1935.—AMERICO PAREDES.)

The Mexico-Texan is one fonny man
Who lives in the region that's north of the Gran';
Of Mexican father, he born in these part,
And sometimes he rues it deep down een hees heart.

For the Mexico-Texan, he no gotta lan';
He stomped on da neck on both sides of the Gran';
The dam gringo lingo he no cannot spik;
It twista da tong and it maka heem sik.
A cit'zen of Texas they say that he ees....
But then—why they call heem da Mexican Grease?
Soft talk and hard actions—he can't understan'—
The Mexico-Texan, he no gotta lan'.

If he cross da reever, eet ees yust as bad;
On high, poleeshed Spanish he braka hees had.
American customs those people no like;
They hate that Miguel shoulda calla heem "Mike."
And Mexican-born, why, they jeer and they hoot,
"Go back to da Gringo! Go leecka hees boot!"
In Texas he's Johnny; in Mexico Juan,
But the Mexico-Texan, he no gotta lan'.

Elections come round and the Gringos are loud;
They pat on hees back and they maka heem proud.
They geeve heem mezcal and da barbacue meat;
They tell heem, "Amigo, we can't be defeat."
But after election, he no gotta fran',
The Mexico-Texan, he no gotta lan'.

Except for a few that in cunning are deft,
He counta so much as a naught to da left.
An' they say everywhere, "He's a burden an' drag—
He plumb like da nigger who no gotta flag;
He no gotta chance....all he got is da hand
To work like da burro—he no gotta lan'."

And only one way can his sorrows all drown;
He'll get drank as hell when next payday come roun',
For he has one advantage of all other man,
Though the Mexico-Texan he no gotta lan'.
He can getta so drunk that he thinka to fly
Both September da Sixteen and Fourth of July.

Figure 22. Facsimile of reprint of poem, "The Mexico-Texan," *Brownsville Herald*, circa 1936. Américo Paredes Papers, Box 12, Folder 1.

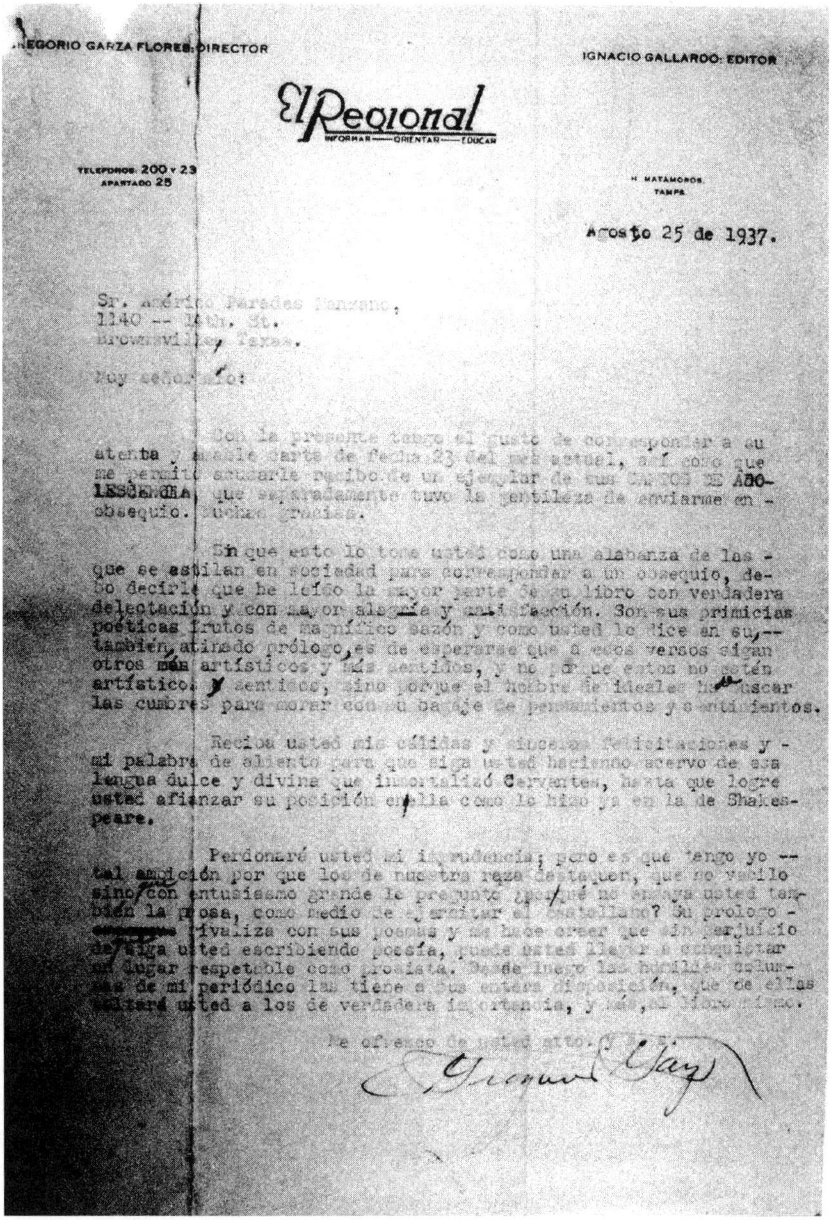

GREGORIO GARZA FLORES: DIRECTOR

IGNACIO GALLARDO: EDITOR

El Regional

INFORMAR — ORIENTAR — EDUCAR

TELEFONOS: 200 Y 23
APARTADO 25

H. MATAMOROS,
TAMPS.

Agosto 25 de 1937.

Sr. Américo Paredes Manzano,
1140 -- 14th. St.
Brownsville, Texas.

Muy señor mío:

Con la presente tengo el gusto de corresponder a su atenta y amable carta de fecha 23 del mes actual, así como que me permito acusarle recibo de un ejemplar de sus CANTOS DE ADOLESCENCIA, que separadamente tuvo la gentileza de enviarme en -obsequio. Muchas gracias.

Sin que esto lo tome usted como una alabanza de las -que se estilan en sociedad para corresponder a un obsequio, debo decirle que he leído la mayor parte de su libro con verdadera delectación y con mayor alegría y satisfacción. Son sus primicias poéticas frutos de magnífico sazón y como usted lo dice en su, --también, atinado prólogo, es de esperarse que a esos versos sigan otros más artísticos y más sentidos, y no porque estos no estén artísticos y sentidos, sino porque el hombre de ideales ha de buscar las cumbres para morar con su bagaje de pensamientos y sentimientos.

Reciba usted mis cálidas y sinceras felicitaciones y -mi palabra de aliento para que siga usted haciendo acervo de esa lengua dulce y divina que inmortalizó Cervantes, hasta que logre usted afianzar su posición en ella como lo hizo ya en la de Shakespeare.

Perdonará usted mi imprudencia; pero es que tengo yo --tal ambición por que los de nuestra raza destaquen, que no vacilo sino con entusiasmo grande le pregunto ¿por qué no ensaya usted también la prosa, como medio de ejercitar el castellano? Su prólogo -[illegible] rivaliza con sus poemas y me hace creer que sin perjuicio de que siga usted escribiendo poesía, puede usted llegar a conquistar un lugar respetable como prosista. Desde luego las humildes columnas de mi periódico las tiene a su entera disposición, que de ellas saltará usted a los de verdadera importancia, y más, al libro mismo.

Me ofrezco de usted atto. y S. S.

Gregorio Garza

Figure 23. Correspondence from Gregorio Garza Flores, Director, *El Regional* (Matamoros, Taumalipas, Mexico), August 25, 1937. Américo Paredes Papers, Box 8, Folder 8.

THE LIBRARY OF THE UNIVERSITY OF TEXAS

DONALD CONEY · LIBRARIAN

AUSTIN · TEXAS

25 de octº, 1937

Sr. Americo Paredes Manzano
1140 14th St.
Brownsville, Texas

Muy estimado joven:

Con verdadera satisfacción he leído el ejemplar de su primer libro de poesías y francamente le felicito por el éxito obtenido. Su esfuerzo es, en verdad, encomioso, y como dijo el redactor del artículo en <u>La Prensa</u> de San Antonio, viene ud. a redimir en parte la inopia literaria de los méxico-tejanos.

Persista ud. en el amplio campo que se ha marcado, seguro de que con la inspiración sincera de su musa desterrada obtendrá el éxito que merece y vindicará el nombre de su raza.

Me repito de ud. su atento servidor y amigo

C. E. Castañeda

C. E. Castañeda
Bibliotecario latinoamericano

CEC:vg

Figure 24. Correspondence from Carlos E. Castañeda, Librarian, University of Texas Library, October 25, 1937. Américo Paredes Papers, Box 8, Folder 8.

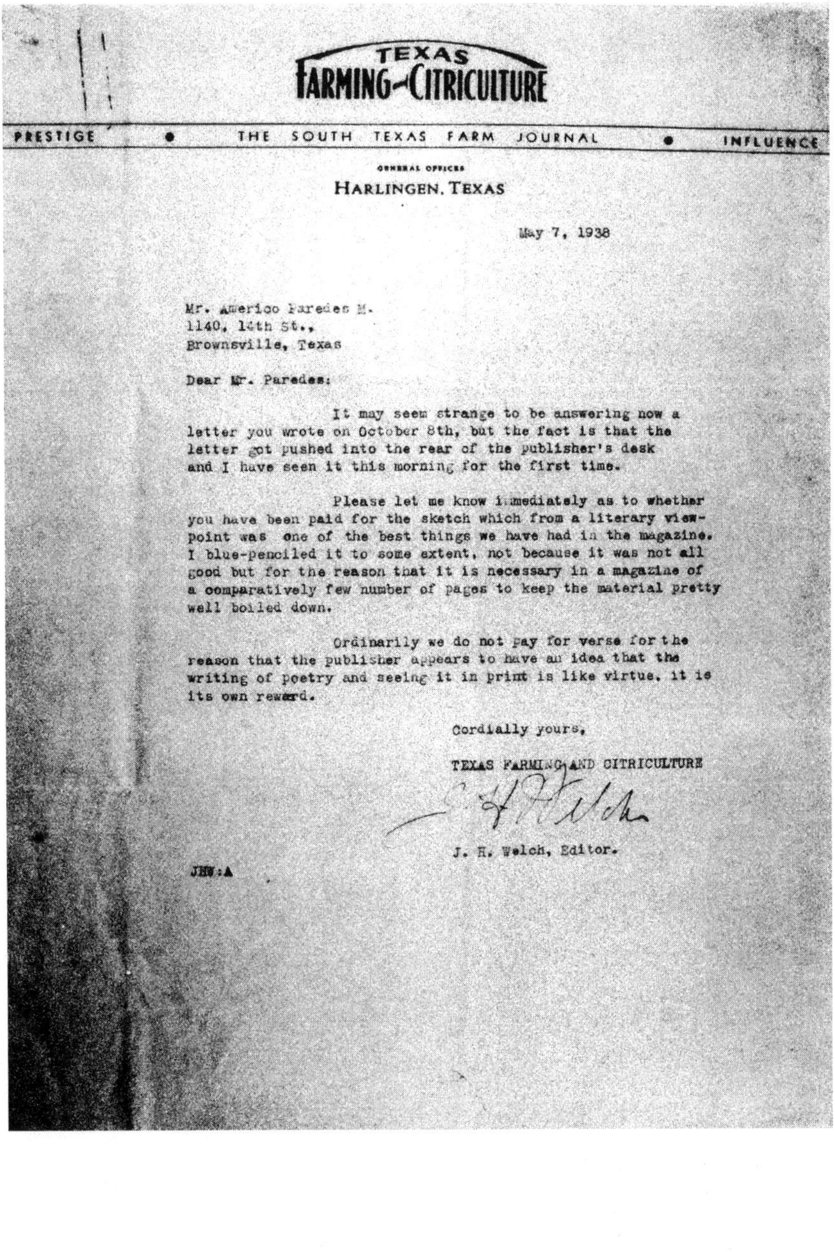

TEXAS
FARMING-CITRICULTURE

PRESTIGE • THE SOUTH TEXAS FARM JOURNAL • INFLUENCE

GENERAL OFFICES
HARLINGEN, TEXAS

May 7, 1938

Mr. Americo Paredes M.
1140, 14th St.,
Brownsville, Texas

Dear Mr. Paredes:

It may seem strange to be answering now a letter you wrote on October 8th, but the fact is that the letter got pushed into the rear of the publisher's desk and I have seen it this morning for the first time.

Please let me know immediately as to whether you have been paid for the sketch which from a literary view-point was one of the best things we have had in the magazine. I blue-penciled it to some extent, not because it was not all good but for the reason that it is necessary in a magazine of a comparatively few number of pages to keep the material pretty well boiled down.

Ordinarily we do not pay for verse for the reason that the publisher appears to have an idea that the writing of poetry and seeing it in print is like virtue, it is its own reward.

Cordially yours,

TEXAS FARMING AND CITRICULTURE

J. H. Welch, Editor.

JHW:A

Figure 25. Correspondence from J.H. Welch, Editor, *Texas Farming and Citriculture*, May 7, 1938. Américo Paredes Papers, Box 8, Folder 8.

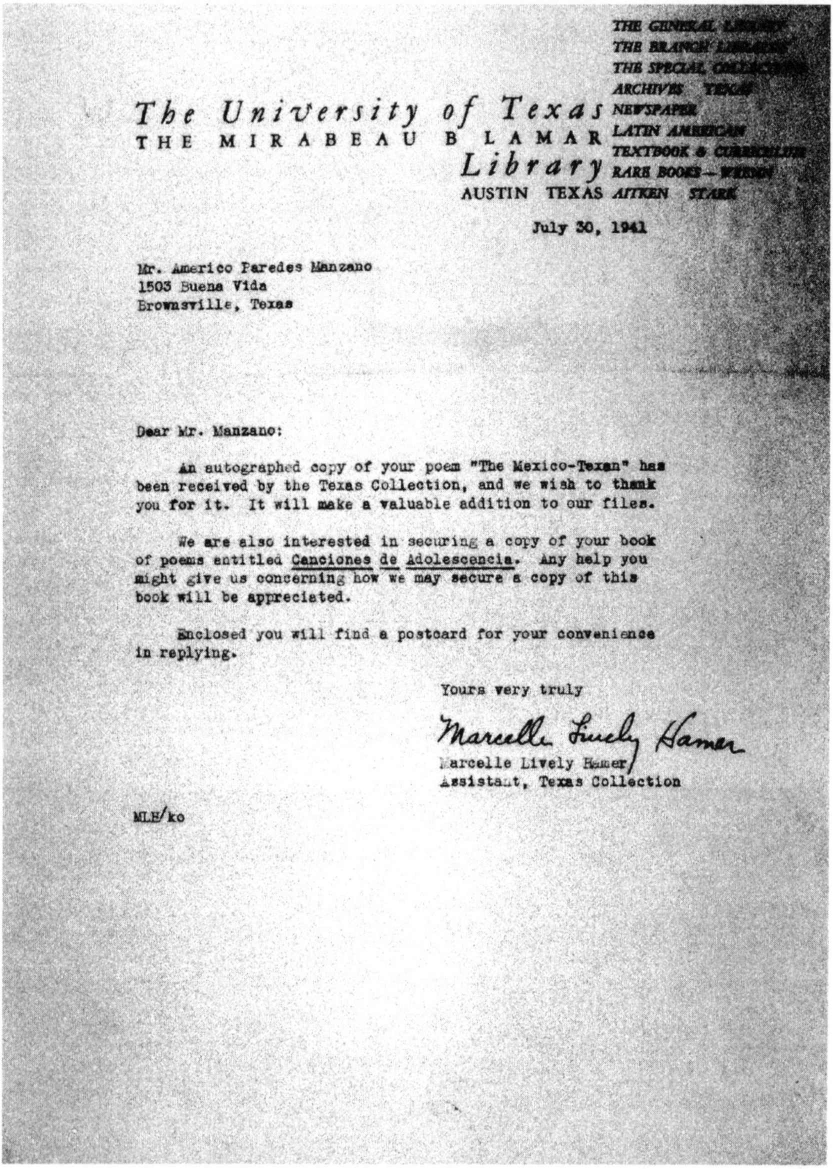

The University of Texas
THE MIRABEAU B LAMAR
Library
AUSTIN TEXAS

THE GENERAL LIBRARY
THE BRANCH LIBRARIES
THE SPECIAL COLLECTIONS
ARCHIVES TEXAS
NEWSPAPER
LATIN AMERICAN
TEXTBOOK & CURRICULUM
RARE BOOKS—WRENN
AITKEN STARK

July 30, 1941

Mr. Americo Paredes Manzano
1503 Buena Vida
Brownsville, Texas

Dear Mr. Manzano:

An autographed copy of your poem "The Mexico-Texan" has been received by the Texas Collection, and we wish to thank you for it. It will make a valuable addition to our files.

We are also interested in securing a copy of your book of poems entitled Canciones de Adolescencia. Any help you might give us concerning how we may secure a copy of this book will be appreciated.

Enclosed you will find a postcard for your convenience in replying.

Yours very truly

Marcelle Lively Hamer
Marcelle Lively Hamer
Assistant, Texas Collection

MLH/ko

Figure 26. Correspondence from Marcelle Lively Hamer, Librarian, Mirabeau Lamar Library, University of Texas at Austin, July 30, 1941. Américo Paredes Papers, Box 8, Folder 8.

Figure 27. Leather jacket for *Cantos de adolescencia* awarded by *The Arizona Quarterly*, circa 1937. Américo Paredes Papers, Box 11, Folder 5.

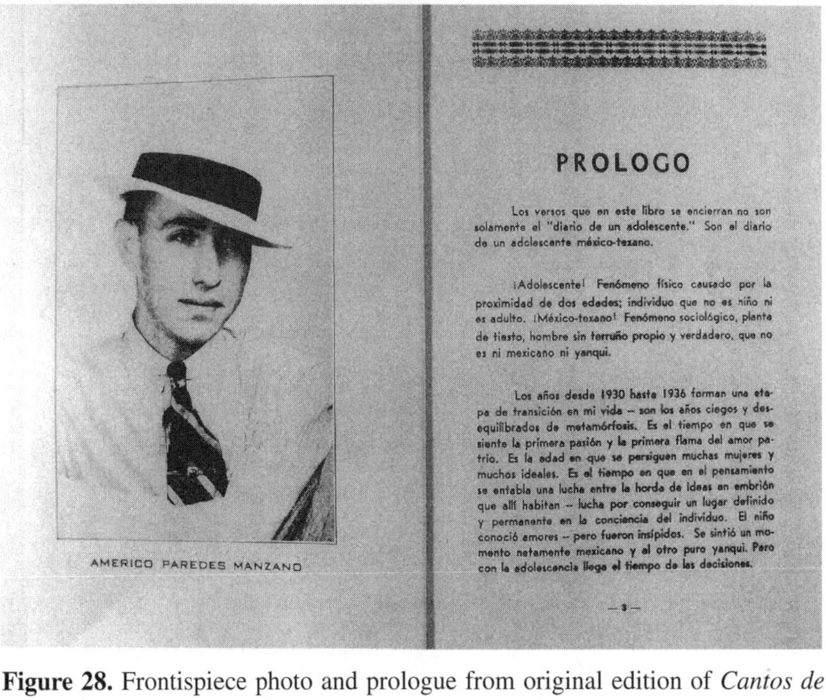

AMERICO PAREDES MANZANO

PROLOGO

Los versos que en este libro se encierran no son solamente el "diario de un adolescente." Son el diario de un adolescente méxico-texano.

¡Adolescente! Fenómeno físico causado por la proximidad de dos edades; individuo que no es niño ni es adulto. ¡México-texano! Fenómeno sociológico, planta de tiesto, hombre sin terruño propio y verdadero, que no es ni mexicano ni yanqui.

Los años desde 1930 hasta 1936 forman una etapa de transición en mi vida – son los años ciegos y desequilibrados de metamórfosis. Es el tiempo en que se siente la primera pasión y la primera flama del amor patrio. Es la edad en que se persiguen muchas mujeres y muchos ideales. Es el tiempo en que en el pensamiento se entabla una lucha entre la horda de ideas en embrión que allí habitan – lucha por conseguir un lugar definido y permanente en la conciencia del individuo. El niño conoció amores – pero fueron insípidos. Se sintió un momento netamente mexicano y el otro puro yanqui. Pero con la adolescencia llega el tiempo de las decisiones.

—3—

Figure 28. Frontispiece photo and prologue from original edition of *Cantos de adolescencia*. Américo Paredes Papers, Box 11, Folder 4.

Figure 29. Photograph of Paredes as a child and sister Blanca on the occasion of Blanca's first communion. Date unknown. Américo Paredes Papers, Special Photograph Box.

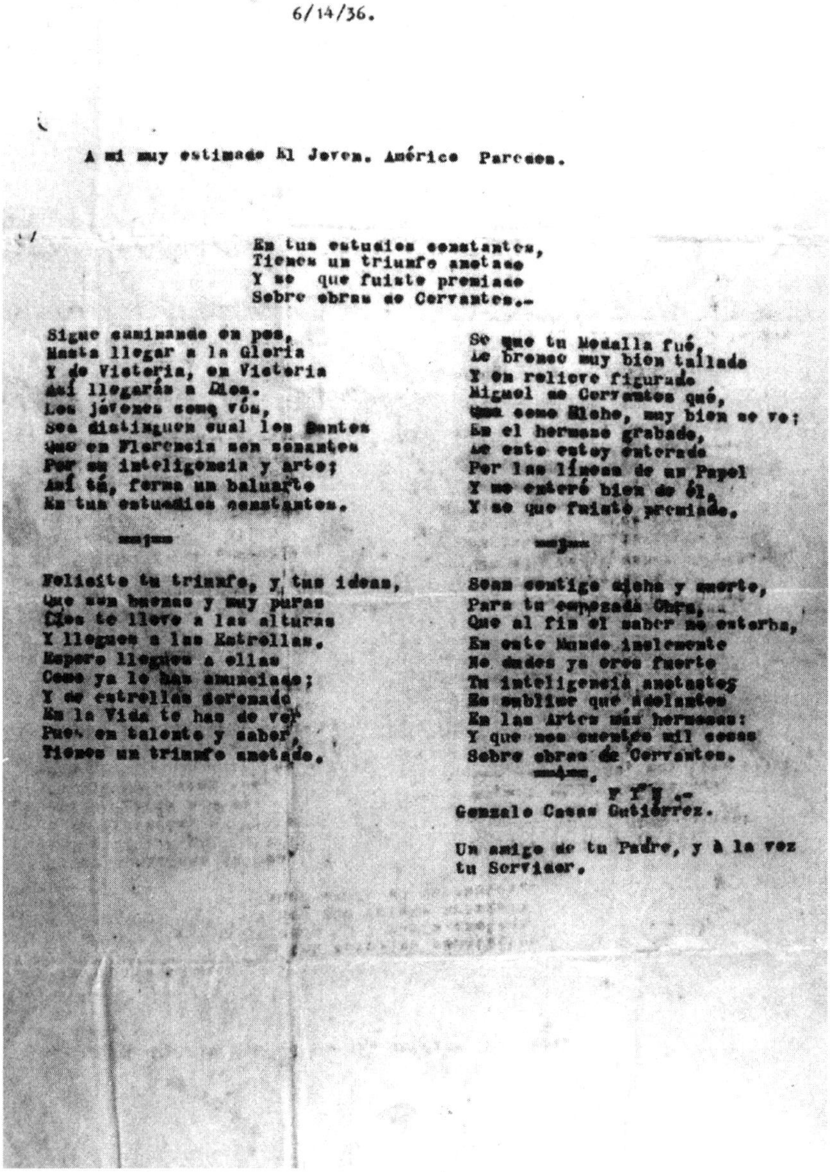

6/14/36.

A mi muy estimado El Joven. Américo Paredes.

En tus estudios constantes,
Tienes un triunfo anotado
Y se que fuiste premiado
Sobre obras de Cervantes.-

Sigue caminando en pos,
Hasta llegar a la Gloria
Y de Victoria, en Victoria
Así llegarás a Dios.
Los jóvenes como vós,
Se distinguen cual los Santos
Que en Florencia son sonantes
Por su inteligencia y arte;
Así tú, forma un baluarte
En tus estuedios constantes.

Felicito tu triunfo, y tus ideas,
Que son buenas y muy puras
Dios te lleve a las alturas
Y llegues a las Estrellas.
Espero llegues a ellas
Como ya lo han anunciado;
Y de estrellas coronado
En la Vida te has de ver
Pues en talento y saber,
Tienes un triunfo anotado.

Se que tu Medalla fué,
De bronce muy bien tallado
Y en relieve figurado
Miguel de Cervantes qué,
Como dicho, muy bien se ve;
En el hermoso grabado,
De esto estoy enterado
Por las líneas de un Papel
Y me enteré bien de él,
Y se que fuiste premiado.

Sean contigo dicha y suerte,
Para tu empezada Obra,
Que al fin el saber no estorba,
En este Mundo inclemente
No dudes ya eres fuerte
Tu inteligencia anotastes
Es sublime que adelantes
En las Artes más hermosas:
Y que nos cuentes mil cosas
Sobre obras de Cervantes.

Gonzalo Casas Gutiérrez.

Un amigo de tu Padre, y à la vez
tu Servidor.

Figure 30. Facsimile of *décima* dedicated to Paredes from Gonzalo Casas Gutiérrez, June 14, 1936. Américo Paredes Papers, Box 5, Folder 3.

Figure 31. Facsimile of poem dedicated to Paredes from cousin Juventino Paredes, date unknown. Américo Paredes Papers, Box 5, Folder 4.

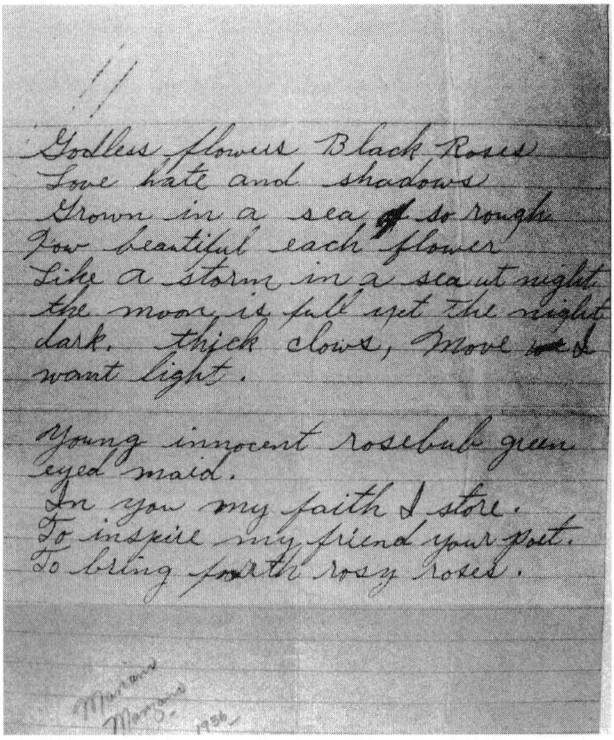

Godless flowers Black Roses
Love hate and shadows
Grown in a sea of so rough
How beautiful each flower
Like a storm in a sea at night
the moon is full yet the night
dark. thick clows, Move I
want light.

Young innocent rosebub green
eyed maid.
In you my faith I store.
To inspire my friend your poet.
To bring forth rosy roses.

Mariano Manzano
1936

Figure 32. Facsimile of poem, "Godless Flowers," by relative Mariano Manzano, circa 1936. Américo Paredes Papers, Box 5, Folder 3.

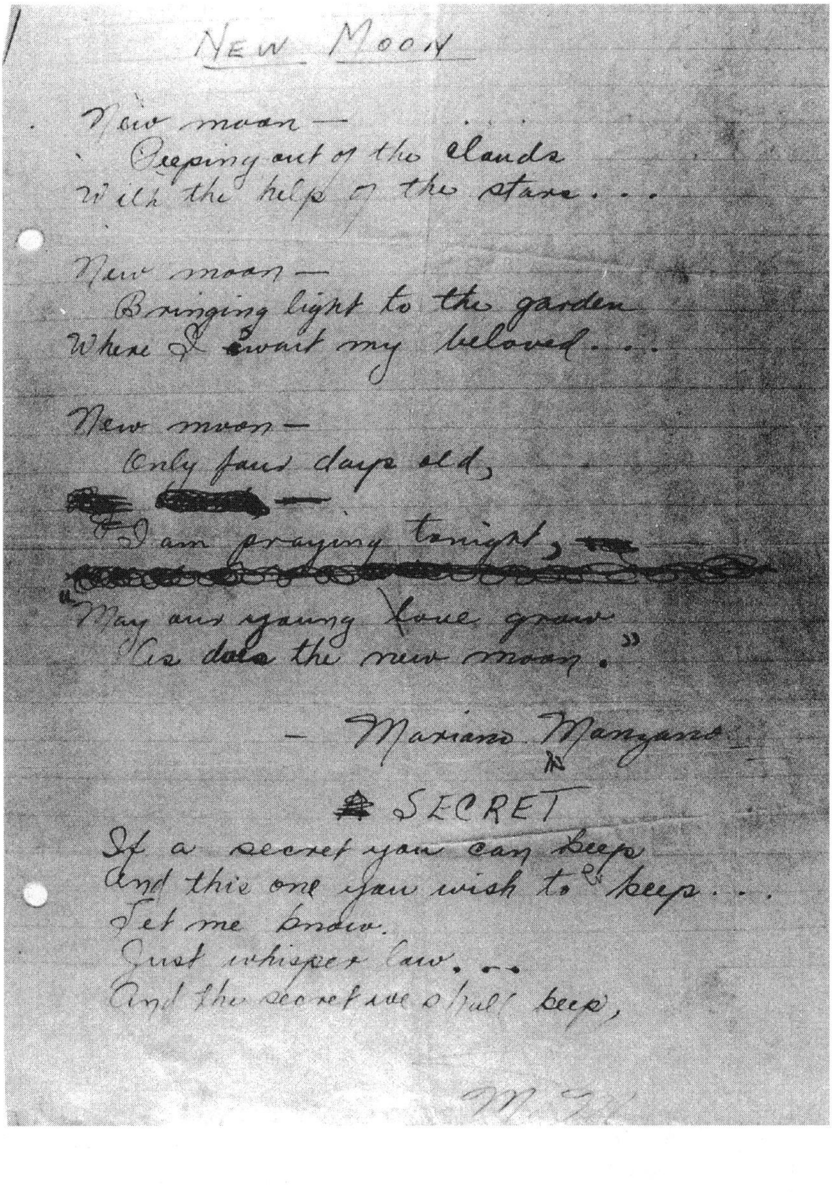
NEW MOON

New moon—
Peeping out of the clouds
With the help of the stars...

New moon—
Bringing light to the garden
Where I await my beloved....

New moon—
Only four days old,
[redacted] —
"I am praying tonight, [redacted]
[redacted]
"May our young love grow
As does the new moon."

— Mariano Manzano

SECRET

If a secret you can keep
And this one you wish to keep...
Let me know.
Just whisper low....
And the secret we shall keep,

M. M.

Figure 33. Facsimile of poem, "New Moon," by Mariano Manzano, circa 1936. Américo Paredes Papers, Box 5, Folder 3.

MI PUEBLO DE AMANECER

A MI AMIGO
SABAS KLAHN

A MI BARRIO,
EL CUATRO VEINTIUNO

Pueblo mío, pueblo mío, multiforme caserío
recostado junto al río
bajo el gris amanecer,
junto al río lento y bruno tienes barrios, uno a uno,
y entre tantos el Veintiuno,
el que a mí me vió crecer.

Pueblo, tú que te lisonjas con palmeras y toronjas,
con tus frailes y tus monjas
y tu iglesia colonial,
con quebrantos y quereres, con cantinas y mujeres,
de pecado capital

¡Tú que cruento y pervertido de mis penas te has reído
porque incógnito y caído
me contemplas, pueblo vil!

Tú que en dulce nigromancia me arrullaste allá en la infancia
y me diste tu fragancia,
¡pueblo vívido y gentil!

Tienes fuertes y raquíticos, hipócritas y críticos,
que te compran con mezcal;
tienes bailes y conciertos; hay riquezas en tus huertos;
llegan naves a tus puertos
por el cielo y por el mar.

Con tus blancas carreteras las distancias aligeras,
tus lozanas gringas güeras
son marfil, oro y azur;
y en tus fiestas y verbenas luces vírgenes morenas
que mis risas y mis penas
las soñaron en el sur.

Eres cierta incertidumbre entre cielo y podredumbre,
del abismo y de la cumbre
el destino te formó;
citadino y campireno, eres yanqui y mexicano;
eres méxico texano,
¡eres pocho como yo!

¡Ah, mi pueblo! No lo ignoro. Yo soy pardo e incoloro,
mas cual pájaro canoro
llevo un canto dentro mí;
ese canto que me llena con su aroma de azucena,
aunque seas tierra ajena,
ese canto es para ti.

Porque a mí me importa un bledo si me apuntas con el dedo,
si de mí murmura quedo
tu "correcta" sociedad,
¡pueblo majo y marrullero! ¡pueblo dulce y romancero!
yo te juro que te quiero,
¡yo te quiero de verdad!

Américo Paredes MANZANO

Brownsville, Texas
Mayo de 1938.

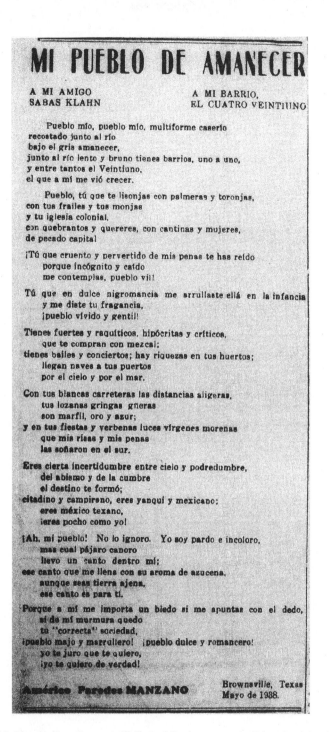

Figure 34. Facsimile of poem, "Mi pueblo de amanecer," by Américo Paredes dedicated to Sabas Klahn, May, 1938. Américo Paredes Papers, Box 12, Folder 1.

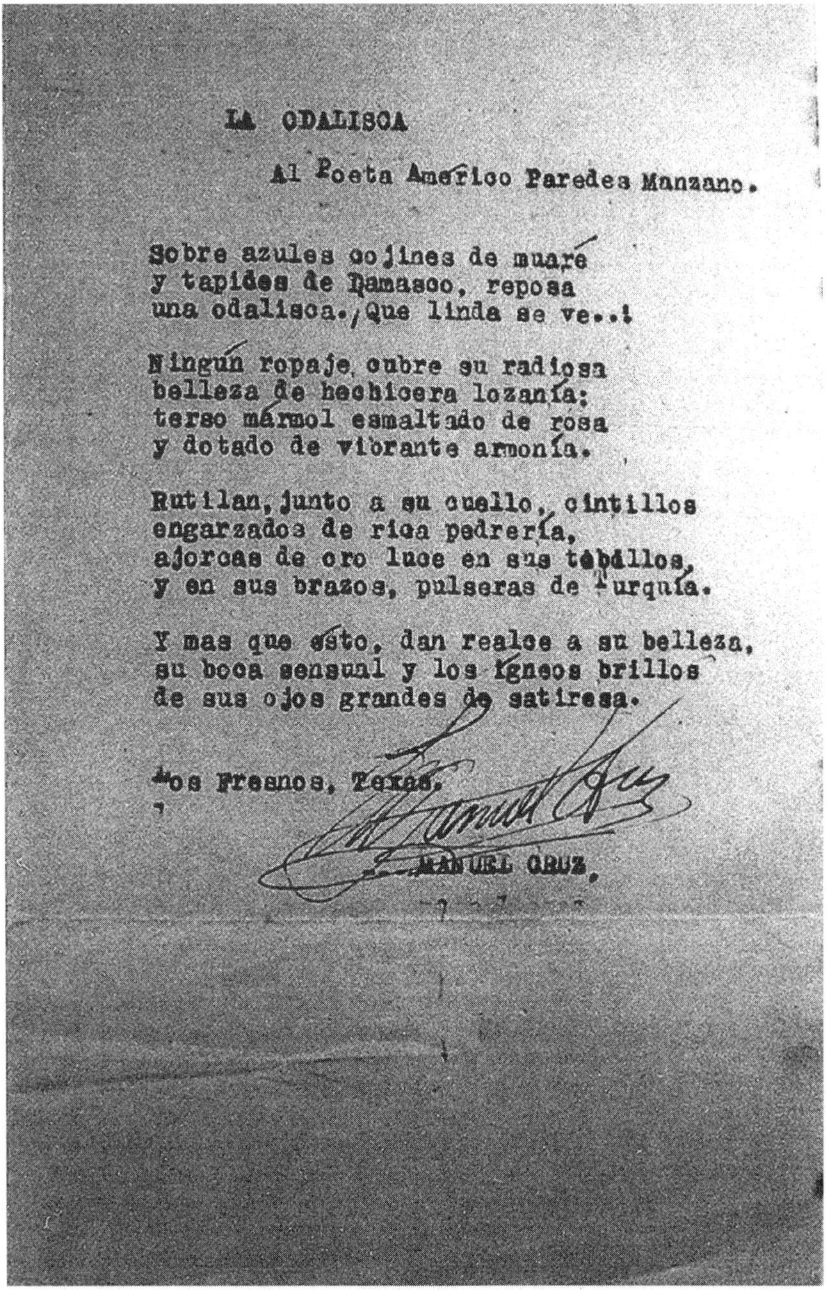

LA ODALISCA

Al Poeta Américo Paredes Manzano.

Sobre azules cojines de muaré
y tapides de Damasco, reposa
una odalisca. ¡Que linda se ve..!

Ningún ropaje cubre su radiosa
belleza de hechicera lozanía;
terso mármol esmaltado de rosa
y dotado de vibrante armonía.

Rutilan, junto a su cuello, cintillos
engarzados de rica pedrería,
ajorcas de oro luce en sus tobillos,
y en sus brazos, pulseras de Turquía.

Y mas que esto, dan realce a su belleza,
su boca sensual y los ígneos brillos
de sus ojos grandes de satiresa.

Los Fresnos, Texas.

MANUEL CRUZ.

Figure 35. Facsimile of poem, "La odalisca," by Manuel Cruz dedicated to Américo Paredes Manzano, circa 1940. Américo Paredes Papers, Box 5, Folder 6.

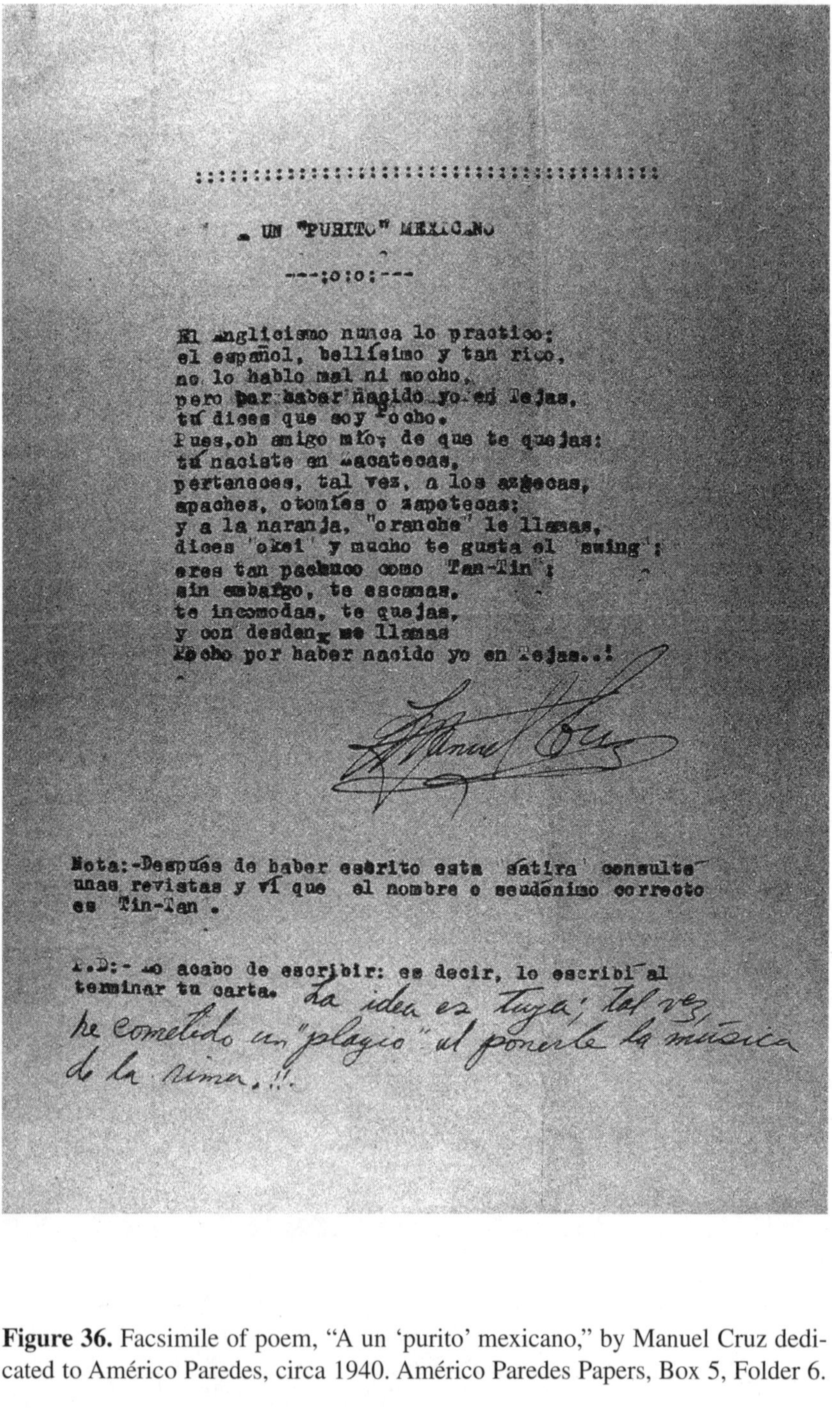

::

A UN "PURITO" MEXICANO

---:o:o:---

El anglicismo nunca lo practico;
el español, bellísimo y tan rico,
no lo hablo mal ni mocho,
pero por haber nacido yo en Tejas,
tú dices que soy Pocho.
Pues,oh amigo mío; de que te quejas:
tú naciste en Zacatecas,
perteneces, tal vez, a los aztecas,
Apaches, otomíes o Zapotecas;
y a la naranja, "oranche" le llamas,
dices "okei" y mucho te gusta el "swing";
eres tan pachuco como "Tan-Tin";
sin embargo, te escamas,
te incomodas, te quejas,
y con desden, me llamas
Pocho por haber nacido yo en Tejas..!

Manuel Cruz

Nota:-Después de haber esbrito esta "sátira" consulté unas revistas y ví que el nombre o seudónimo correcto es "Tin-Tan".

P.D:- Lo acabo de escribir: es decir, lo escribí al terminar tu carta. La idea es tuya; tal vez he cometido un "plagio" al poner le la música de la rima..!!.

Figure 36. Facsimile of poem, "A un 'purito' mexicano," by Manuel Cruz dedicated to Américo Paredes, circa 1940. Américo Paredes Papers, Box 5, Folder 6.

26 de febrero de 1943

Mi estimado Manuel:

Espero que te encuentres bien y que la musa lirica siga batiendo sus alas sobre tu frente. Yo por mi parte poco tiempo he tenido para la pobrecita y menos para su rival, mi otra amada, la musica. Pero pasando marzo espero terminar las clases de dibujo mecanico que estoy tomando y ojala tenga mas tiempo para las cosas que embellecen el alma. A proposito, los primeros dias de marzo seran los Dias del Charro en esta ciudad. De seguro que daras una vuelta por estos contornos a gozar del colorido de un mexicanismo exuberante aunque sintetico.

Bolviendo a la literatura, la guerra disminuye sus brillos. La incertidumbre del futuro y la bestialidad del presente no son terreno propicio para las flores del corazon. Hay veces que creo que pensar en estos tiempos en la poesia es como cantar y reir en un funeral. Hay tantos de los nuestros exponiendo sus vidas en las duras realidades de la guerra. En la negra noche del cataclismo por que pasamos, mi canto se me parece una debil voz en la obscuridad--

Voz en la obscuridad que vas cantando
una cancion de luces y alegria
sin pensar en que tarda el nuevo dia,
?vendra el amanecer? !quien sabe cuando!
!oh, mi inutil cancion! no esta a tu mando
acallar con tu debil melodia
el terrible estertor de la agonia
de los jovenes labios escapando.
Es obscura la noche y tormentosa,
la mancha de Cain quedo estampada
en la faz de la tierra dolorosa,
voz en la obscuridad, cesa tu canto,
porque la humanidad es desdichada--
muere su juventud--!y sufre tanto!

Es dificil en estos tiempos mantener viva la debil flama de la inquietud divina, palido fuego que se agita con el furor de los ciclones y que busca expirar. Pero hay que atizarlo; hay que buscar pasto para sus llamas para que sea una hoguera como fue en los locos dias de nuestra juventud. Yo quisiera tener tiempo, mucho tiempo, aunque fuera aun mas pobre que Job. Entonces, siendo dueno de mi mismo formaria un circulo literario, un circulo en el que en verdad se elevara el alma, cantando toda la vida. Pero es imposible. Todos nosotros somos esclavos del mundo y sus obligaciones y tenemos que hacer solamente lo que podamos. Y si podemos vernos de vez en cuando y leer versos. Hasta la vista, entonces, Manuel, y sigue escribiendo en la obscuridad de esta noche feraz por la que pasamos. Tendra que amanecer.

Tu amigo,

Figure 37. Facsimile of correspondence from Américo Paredes to Manuel Cruz, February 26, 1943. Américo Paredes Papers, Box 5, Folder 6.

1556 Garfield
Brownsville, Texas
7 de enero de 1943

Mi estimado Manuel:--

Recibi tu carta y tambien el soneto incluso, que me fue tan inmerecido como grato. Yo tambien te deseo un feliz ano nuevo. Ano nuevo, vida nueva, dice el vulgo. No es nueva nunca la vida, ni tampoco es vieja. Es inmutable, imperecedera, e inmarcesible. Somos nosotros los que cambiamos, hasta que llegamos a decir como Cortinas:

"Un ano mas, !que largos son los anos!
para el pobre que mira en lontananza
un porvenir de amargos desenganos
que marchita la flor de su esperanza."

Tiene algo lo amargo que es casi dulzura, ya sea en un vaso de licor o en el episodio de una vida. Por eso en el mundo hay tantos beodos y tantos poetas. La amargura es la musa mas sincera y con ella se siente mas hondo. Esa es la razon por la cual de todos tus versos prefiero el Romance de Amargura. Alli esta el dolor sencillo, el alma desnuda como una espada--sin el envaine encrustado del artificio lujoso. Escribe muchos poemas como el Romance de Amargura.

Volviendo a lo del domingo 17, ya estamos de acuerdo de vernos todos en mi casa a la una de la tarde. El agasajo tomara forma de una comida que se verificara en un restoran en Matamoros. Escribeme si tienes pasaporte y si no es asi arreglaremos para hacer la comida en Brownsville. La guerra ha disminuido nuestro circulo y no somos mas que cinco los que nos reuniremos contigo el domingo. Faltaran entre nosotros companeros como Antonio Arangua, Mariano Manzano, Eleazar Paredes, Jose Pena y otros--todos amantes de la poesia, la musica y el arte, pero que se encuentran en estos momentos o enel ejercito o en la marina. Solo quedamos unos cuantos, pero estaran presentes en primer termino Sabas Klahn y Roberto Ramirez, de quienes habras leido algunas lineas en mis Cantos. Los dos tienen muchos versos y los de Klahn se destacan por su musica y su forma impecable mientras que los de Ramirez por su acento melancolico y su estilo peculiar. Tambien estara con nosotros Adan Ramos, otro amante de la rima y tambien el Sr. Oscar J. del Castillo, director de El Heraldo de Brownsville, quien me ha dicho publicara algunos poemas tuyos en breves dias. Nosotros cinco contigo seremos seis, no el numero para un gran banquete pero si para una comida intima en la que podremos discutir cosas de arte y conocernos todos mejor. Con ocasion de la referida cena y las libaciones que en ella habra, asi como en contestacion de tu brindis y tu soneto, te dedico el siguiente, algo caprichoso pero sincero:--

BRINDIS

Ambrosia fatal, nectar divino,
miel que nos satisface y embelesa,
cuestas menos y vales mas que el vino,
!o plebeya y magnifica cerveza!
Seamos financiero--campesino--
tu nos prestas donaire y sutileza,
nos inspiras el verbo diamantino,
traes ilusiones mil a la cabeza.

Que importa que me digan los galenos
que eres un cruel veneno que me mata--
sea su voluntad--un loco menos. . .
?Quién se niega a bebida tan galana?
Sirvele, cantinera; sirve ingrata--
!Aunque me tenga que morir manana!

Figure 38. Facsimile of correspondence from Américo Paredes to Manuel Cruz with poem, "Brindis," dedicated to Cruz, January 7, 1943. Américo Paredes Papers, Box 5, Folder 6.

P A S A T I E M P O
L I R I C O

Cariñosamente a mis buenos
amigos, Américo y Sabas...

En una orgiástica fiesta
de placer, vino y embeleso,
derrochan sus horas de ocio
cuatro cultos caballeros,
cuatro empedernidos amantes
de la Belleza y del Verso.
Con mélicos ditirambos,
con suspiros y con poemas
y exóticas libaciones
tratan de revivir muertos,
(Caramba..no os espanteis..!)
revivir muertos anhelos.

Ironías..! Muchos beben
para olvidar sentimientos,
penas o negras desdichas:
más estos caballeros,
estos empedernidos amantes
de la Belleza y del Verso,
liban para recordar
aquellos sus buenos tiempos,
aquella su juventud
llena de encantos risueños:
y asi, efusivos brindan
por la magia del Recuerdo.

Exhaustos, es decir, beodos,
se retiran del recuerdo,
por no decir del licor,
y practicando el zigzagueo
como ejercicio gimnástico,
van a su hogar aquellos
cuatro cultos caballeros,
cuatro empedernidos amantes
de la Belleza y del Verso..!

Los Fresnos: 2 de enero de 1944.

Figure 39. Facsimile of poem, "Pasatiempo lírico," by Manuel Cruz dedicated to Américo Paredes, January 2, 1944. Américo Paredes Papers, Box 5, Folder 6.

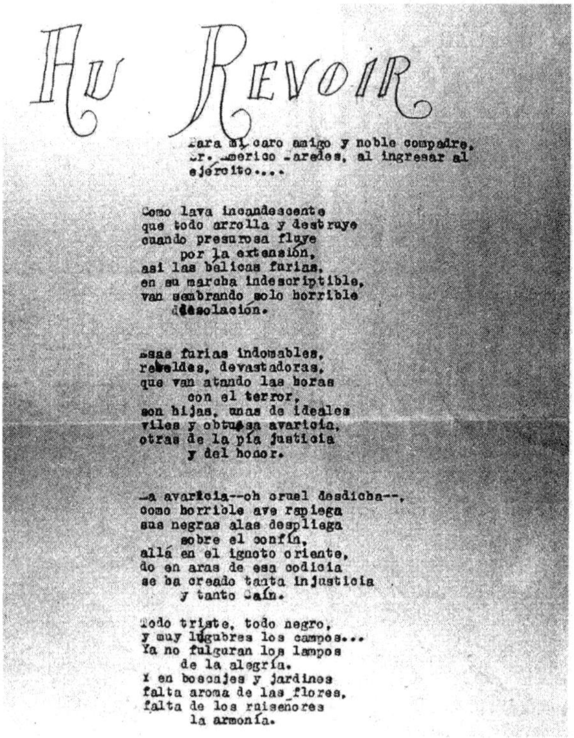

Au Revoir

Para mi caro amigo y noble compadre,
Sr. Américo Paredes, al ingresar al
ejército....

Como lava incandescente
que todo arrolla y destruye
cuando presurosa fluye
por la extensión,
así las bélicas furias,
en su marcha indescriptible,
van sembrando sólo horrible
desolación.

Esas furias indomables,
rebeldes, devastadoras,
que van atando las horas
con el terror,
son hijas, unas de ideales
viles y obtusa avaricia,
otras de la pía justicia
y del honor.

La avaricia--oh cruel desdicha--,
como horrible ave rapiega
sus negras alas despliega
sobre el confín,
allá en el ignoto oriente,
do en aras de esa codicia
se ha creado tanta injusticia
y tanto Caín.

Todo triste, todo negro,
y muy lúgubres los campos...
Ya no fulguran los lampos
de la alegría.
Y en boscajes y jardines
falta aroma de las flores,
falta de los ruiseñores
la armonía.

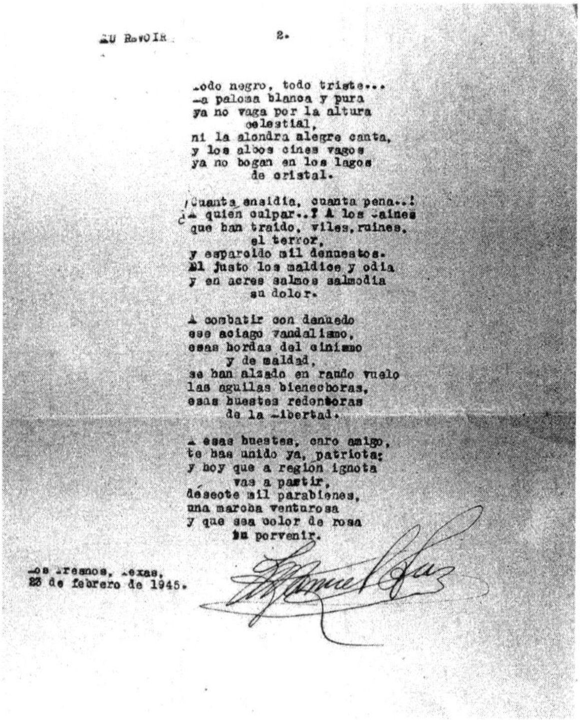

AU REVOIR 2.

Todo negro, todo triste...
La paloma blanca y pura
ya no vaga por la altura
celestial,
ni la alondra alegre canta,
y los albos cines vagos
ya no bogan en los lagos
de cristal.

¡Cuanta ensidia, cuanta pena..!
¿A quién culpar..? A los Caínes
que han traído, viles, ruines,
el terror,
y esparcido mil denuestos.
El justo los maldice y odia
y en acres salmos salmodia
su dolor.

A combatir con denuedo
ese aciago vandalismo,
esas hordas del cinismo
y de maldad,
se han alzado en raudo vuelo
las águilas bienechoras,
esas huestes redentoras
de la Libertad.

A esas huestes, caro amigo,
te has unido ya, patriota;
y hoy que a región ignota
vas a partir,
deséote mil parabienes,
una marcha venturosa
y que sea color de rosa
tu porvenir.

Los Fresnos, Texas,
23 de febrero de 1945.

Figure 40. Facsimile of poem, "Au revoir," by Manuel Cruz dedicated to Américo Paredes, circa 1945. Américo Paredes Papers, Box 5, Folder 6.

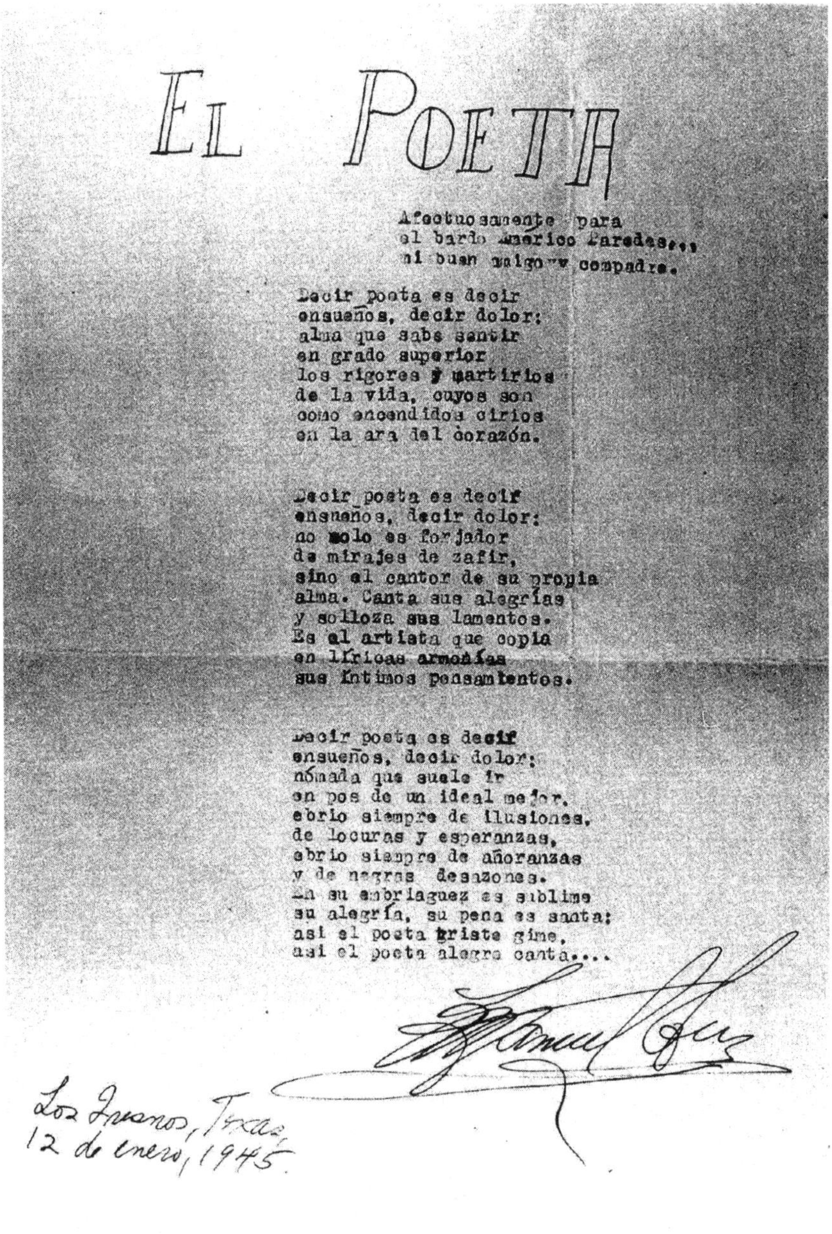

EL POETA

Afectuosamente para
el bardo Américo Paredes...
mi buen amigo y compadre.

Decir poeta es decir
ensueños, decir dolor;
alma que sabe sentir
en grado superior
los rigores y martirios
de la vida, cuyos son
como encendidos cirios
en la ara del corazón.

Decir poeta es decir
ensueños, decir dolor;
no solo es forjador
de mirajes de zafir,
sino el cantor de su propia
alma. Canta sus alegrías
y solloza sus lamentos.
Es el artista que copia
en líricas armonías
sus íntimos pensamientos.

Decir poeta es decir
ensueños, decir dolor;
nómada que suele ir
en pos de un ideal mejor,
ebrio siempre de ilusiones,
de locuras y esperanzas,
ebrio siempre de añoranzas
y de negras desazones.
En su embriaguez es sublime
su alegría, su pena es santa;
asi el poeta triste gime,
asi el poeta alegre canta....

Manuel Cruz

Los Fresnos, Texas,
12 de enero, 1945.

Figure 41. Facsimile of poem, "El poeta," by Manuel Cruz dedicated to Américo Paredes by Manuel Cruz, January 12, 1945. Américo Paredes Papers, Box 5, Folder 6.

PRÓLOGO

He venido a estas páginas solamente a presentar al autor. Seré breve.

Nació Manuel Cruz el 12 de agosto de 1918 en la ciudad de [redacted] Victoria Tejas, siendo su padre originario de Laredo, Tejas, y su madre de Nuevo Laredo, Tamaulipas. ~~En Taft~~, Manuel fué a la escuela y aprendió muchas cosas. Aprendió a hablar inglés, estudió los capítulos más negros de la historia de México, y aprendió a cantar "Beautiful Texas". Al mismo tiempo ensayaba el español al calor del hogar. Escribió muchas poemas, que a él se le antojó fueran todas hembras, y comenzó varias novelas donde escribía hermano sin "h".

El futuro poeta fue creciendo y a su debido tiempo tuvo suficiente oportunidad de ser excluído de restaurants, de ser negado la entrada a hoteles y de poder votar por los candidatos del partido demócrata. Si no se valió de tan magníficas oportunidades tal vez fue porque no las supo ~~agradecer~~. aprovechar.

Con tan persistente y dolorosa recordatoria, con esta saña nacida de antiguos rencores y alimentada por la estupidez y la ignorancia, difícil sería para el mexico-tejano olvidar su origen, su sangre y su nativo idioma, aunque así lo quisiera. Y raras veces lo quiere. He aquí que el mexico-tejano no solo conserve viva su lengua original sino que también ensaye en ella la literatura.

?Es "antiamericano" el mexicano de Tejas porque habla el español? Vive en paz, obedece las leyes del país y trabaja mucho. Con su trabajo ha hecho desaparecer grandes extensiones del chaparral para luego hacer florecer la tierra, enriqueciendo a sus dueños. Ha mandado a sus hijos a la escuela a aprender inglés y a las fuerzas armadas a defender a la unión americana.

Pero la lengua de sus abuelos, maltrecha y apochada como la habla, sigue siendo su lengua. Y esta insistencia en no olvidar el español es de donde nacen todas las distinciones y los prejuicios en contra de él. No es el color, ya que el indio "americano" goza de todos los privilegios de los "blancos".

En este ambiente nació y creció Manuel Cruz, autor de Remanso Azul. Y por haber nacido en Tejas habrá quien le llame pocho y encuentre mucho que criticar a estos sus versos. Quizás tal crítica venga ¡oh honor! de la Capital. Con "La Capital" se entiende naturalmente La Ciudad de México o Mexico City, como le dicen muchos de sus habitantes. Es "la capital" para el mexico-tejano la ciudad encantada, la ciudad del ensueño y los palacios, donde palpita el corazón y el cerebro de su raza.

Llega a ella, la conoce. ¡Qué desilusión! Encuentra que en la Ciudad de los Tarzanes hay más pachucos que charros, más swing que mariachis. Que se dice oranch, okei y highball y que se baila estilo jitterbug en Xochimilco. Llega a pensar que ya está seca la misma fuente de donde su incipiente personalidad proviene. Y pensativo murmurará: ?Dónde estará Vasconcelos?

Figure 42. Facsimile of first draft of Américo Paredes' Prologue to *Romanso azul* by Manuel Cruz, May 24, 1944. Américo Paredes Papers, Box 5, Folder 6.

Form 2147

AMERICAN RED CROSS

Seoul
28 de abril de 1948
3 p.m.

Mi Nenita querida,

En verdad que el correo esta algo loco. Hace dos dias recibi tu carta del 21, dos del 22, y una del 23. Hoy recibi tu carta del dia 20. Pero, tarde o temprano, tan xxxxx deseada como siempre. Me desilusione un poquitoxxxxxx nada mas, pues ya habia recibido tu carta del 23, en contestacion a la mia del 20, en contestacion a la tuya del 14. Y creia que esta seria del 24. . .con nuevas noticias. Pero xx ahoga nai.

Asi es que el dia 20 se levanto a las 10 y media mi Nena, la muy floja. Va a tener que cambiar mucho cuando se case, pues no podra hacer las tortillas de harina para las 6 a.m. levantandose a esas horas. . . . . la verdad es que en los dias de fiesta yo creo que ni tu ni yo. . . . bueno, no sirve ponerse a soñar despierto uno tan lejos. Pero, como decia un joven poeta, el malogrado Manuel Cruz, muchacho de origen humilde pero de mucha inspiracion, amigo mio que murio a los 25 años, de cancer:--

"!Que dulce es soñar despierto!
Concebir bellos anhelos,
Como la ilusion azules
Y vastos como los cielos,
Soñar asi no es locura,
Solo es dar con emocion
Alas al pensamiento
Y ventura al corazon."

Cuando vayamos a Texas tenemos que buscar la familia de Manuel. Quisiera recoger sus versos, editarlos y publicarlos, aunque fuera de mi propio bolsillo. No debiera pasar a la nada, como la flor de Gray's Elegy, "born to blush unseen and waste its sweetness on the desert air."

Bueno, dejare esto para despues y contestare tu carta. Si vieras tu también la manera que me paso yo los dias esperando carta tuya. Hoy, para las once ya no pude trabajar, pues el Area office esta cerrado en xxx las tardes los miercoles. Invente un asunto para ir al Area office y recoger el correo. Nadie me xxxxx creyo. Todos sabian bien a que iba. Me dices que Art me compro el exposure meter. Que bueno, pues no sera facil que venga otra ganga de esas por mucho tiempo. Aqui en Seoul hay los mismos meters, pero estan a 13 dolares todavia. No hablaron de Tokio el 21. El 23 si hablaron, Dick y Tobe, pero no Art. Ayer, el 27, hable yo y logre platicar con Art, pero no me dijo nada del EM. Creo que manana hablare otra vez y le dare las gracias. Tan facil que es hablar a Tokio. . .pero no puedo hacerlo contigo. Que daria por oir tu voz, aunque fuera por telefono. No me mandes los bulletins, mi amor. Leelos tu; si ves que son nada mas "rutina", no me los mandes. Guardalos mejor. Que ya se fue Witkop. No era mal chico, un poco "stuffy" y estupido, pero no malo de verdad. A nosotros en PRO nos dio mucha lata por lo de los uniformes. Pero el sentia que estaba haciendo su deber. Cuando volvi de EEUU me dio muy mal "billet." Alli tambien fue su caracter. Es debil y les tenia miedo a los del ejercito. Ni para el hablaba. No conozco muy bien a Ruth Crunden. Las pocas veces que he tratado con ella me ha tratado muy bien. ?Ella es la personnel director ahora?

Figure 43. Facsimile of correspondence from Américo Paredes to his wife Amelia, with gloss of Manuel Cruz' poem, April 28, 1948. Américo Paredes Papers, Box 1, Folder 1.

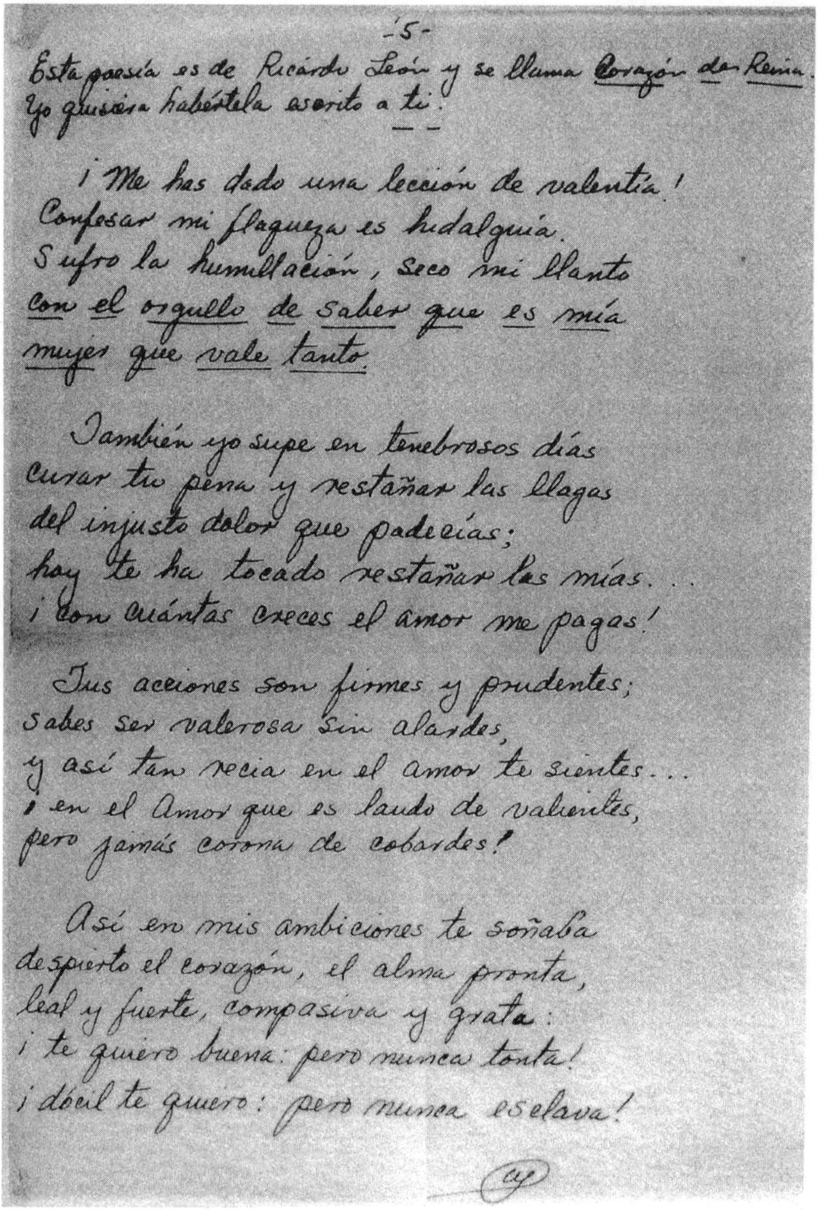

-5-

Esta poesía es de Ricardo León y se llama Corazón de Reina.
Yo quisiera habértela escrito a ti.

¡Me has dado una lección de valentía!
Confesar mi flaqueza es hidalguía.
Sufro la humillación, seco mi llanto
con el orgullo de saber que es mía
mujer que vale tanto.

También yo supe en tenebrosos días
curar tu pena y restañar las llagas
del injusto dolor que padecías;
hoy te ha tocado restañar las mías...
¡Con cuántas creces el amor me pagas!

Tus acciones son firmes y prudentes;
sabes ser valerosa sin alardes,
y así tan recia en el amor te sientes...
¡en el Amor que es lauro de valientes,
pero jamás corona de cobardes!

Así en mis ambiciones te soñaba
despierto el corazón, el alma pronta,
leal y fuerte, compasiva y grata:
¡te quiero buena: pero nunca tonta!
¡dócil te quiero: pero nunca esclava!

Figure 44. Facsimile of correspondence from Américo Paredes to his wife Amelia, with gloss of Manuel Cruz' poem, February 8, 1948. Américo Paredes Papers, Box 1, Folder 1.

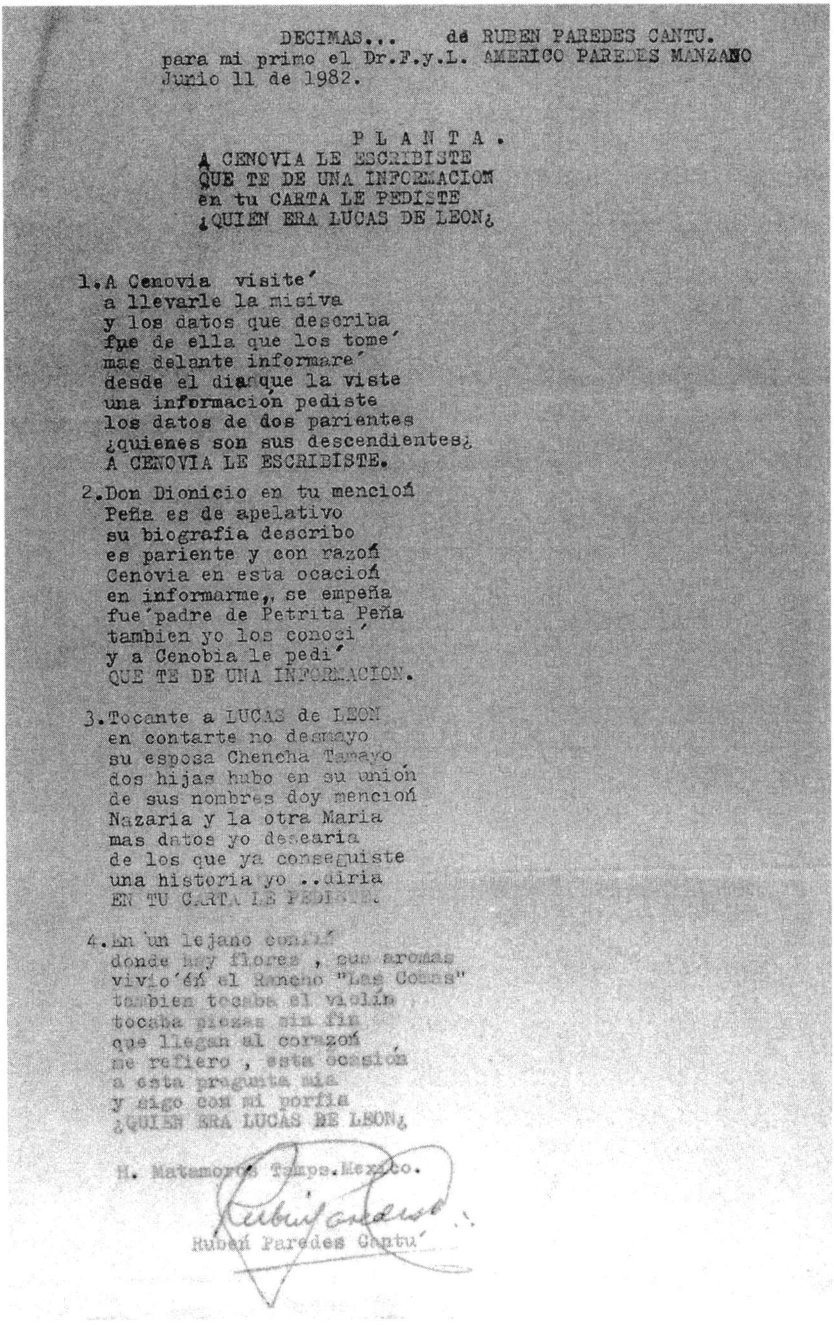
DECIMAS... de RUBEN PAREDES CANTU.
para mi primo el Dr.F.y.L. AMERICO PAREDES MANZANO
Junio 11 de 1982.

P L A N T A .
A CENOVIA LE ESCRIBISTE
QUE TE DE UNA INFORMACION
en tu CARTA LE PEDISTE
¿QUIEN ERA LUCAS DE LEON¿

1. A Cenovia visite´
a llevarle la misiva
y los datos que describa
fue de ella que los tome´
mas delante informare´
desde el dia que la viste
una informacion pediste
los datos de dos parientes
¿quienes son sus descendientes¿
A CENOVIA LE ESCRIBISTE.

2. Don Dionicio en tu mencioń
Peña es de apelativo
su biografia describo
es pariente y con razoń
Cenovia en esta ocacioń
en informarme, se empeña
fue´padre de Petrita Peña
tambien yo los conoci´
y a Cenobia le pedi´
QUE TE DE UNA INFORMACION.

3. Tocante a LUCAS de LEON
en contarte no desmayo
su esposa Chencha Tamayo
dos hijas hubo en su unión
de sus nombres doy mencioń
Nazaria y la otra Maria
mas datos yo desearia
de los que ya conseguiste
una historia yo ..diria
EN TU CARTA LE PEDISTE.

4. En un lejano confiń
donde hay flores , sus aromas
vivio´eń el Rancho "Las Comas"
tambien tocaba el violín
tocaba piezas sin fin
que llegan al corazoń
me refiero , esta ocasión
a esta pregunta mia
y sigo con mi porfia
¿QUIEN ERA LUCAS DE LEON¿

H. Matamoros Tamps.Mexico.

Rubén Paredes Cantu´

Figure 45. Facsimile of *décima* by cousin Rubén Paredes Cantú dedicated to Américo Paredes, June 11, 1982. Américo Paredes Papers, Box 5, Folder 6.

Figure 46. Facsimile of lyrics and musical score for "Tarde de otoño," by Américo Paredes, date unknown. Américo Paredes Papers, Box 5, Folder 12.

Figure 47. Facsimile of musical score for "Flor de burdel," by Américo Paredes, date unknown. Américo Paredes Papers, Box 78, Folder 8.

FLOR DE BURDEL

Tango - L. y M. de A. Paredes M.

Pobre mujer. Mujer de los burdeles,
vestida y coloreada cual el payo,
ocultas tu desdicha y tu desmayo
tras juergas, carcajadas y oropeles,
tras juergas, carcajadas y oropeles.

He venido a comprarte con dinero,
sirena del pantano, sé que tú eres
la maldita entre todas las mujeres,
sin embargo te busco y te deseo,
sin embargo te busco y te deseo.

Flor de burdel, deshojada por los crueles,
flor de burdel, sin aromas y sin mieles,
he de olvidar en tus brazos mis quereres,
y en tu maldad, la maldad de otras mujeres,
marchita flor, flor de burdel.

Sé muy bien que eres de todos,
que te compro con dinero,
sin embargo yo te busco
porque sé que no me engañas,
como me engañaron otras,
flor de burdel.

Figure 48. Facsimile of lyrics for "Flor de burdel," by Américo Paredes, date unknown. Américo Paredes Papers, Box 78, Folder 8.

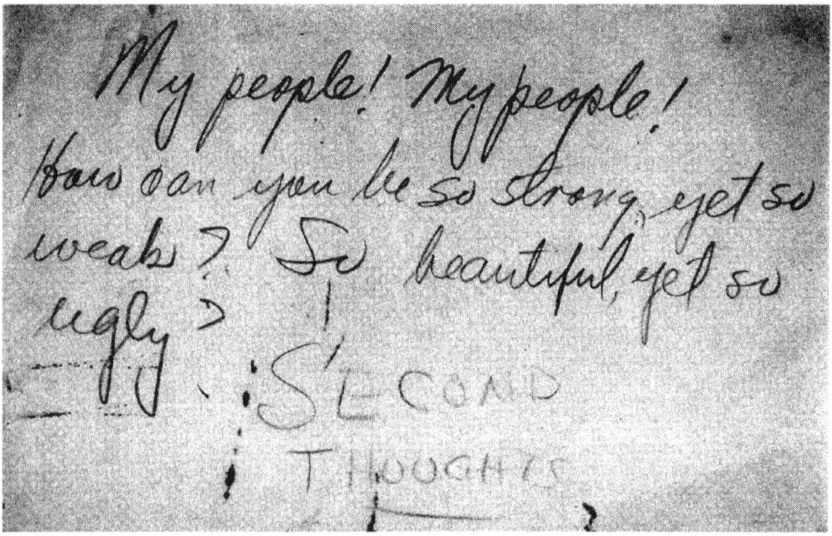

Figure 49. Facsimile of handwritten note by Américo Paredes, no date. Américo Paredes Papers, Box 7, Folder 17.

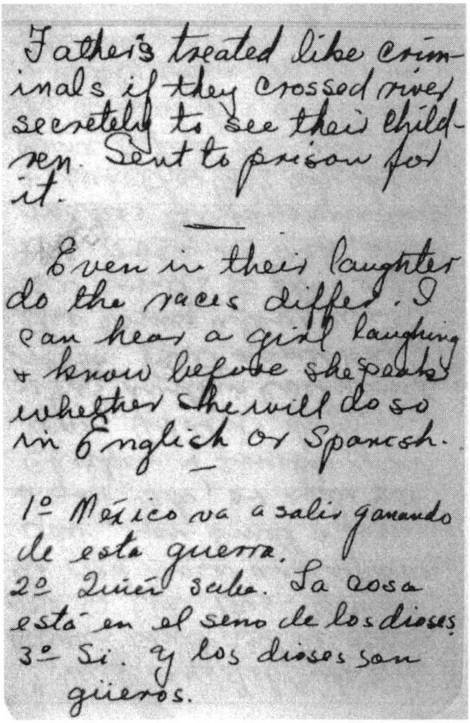

Father's treated like criminals if they crossed river secretely to see their children. Sent to prison for it.

—

Even in their laughter do the races differ. I can hear a girl laughing + know before she speaks whether she will do so in English or Spanish.

—

1º México va a salir ganando de esta guerra.
2º Quién sabe. La cosa está en el seno de los dioses
3º Si. Y los dioses son güeros.

Figure 50. Facsimile of handwritten note by Américo Paredes, no date. Américo Paredes Papers, Box 7, Folder 17.

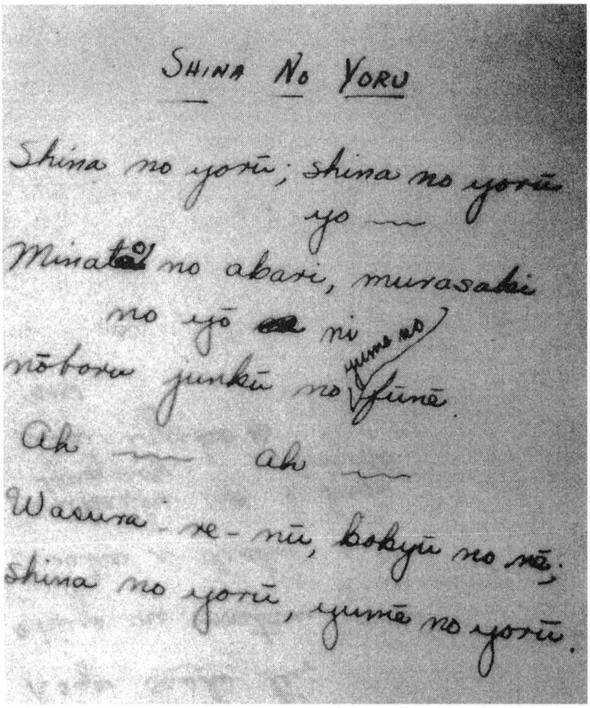

SHINA NO YORU

Shina no yorū; shina no yorū
yo ~~
Minato no akari, murasaki
no yō ni
nōboru junkū no yume no fūnē.
Ah ~~ ah ~~
Wasura-re-nū, kokyū no nē,
Shina no yorū, yumē no yorū.

Figure 51. Facsimile of handwritten lyric, "Shina No Yoru," in phonetic Japanese by Américo Paredes, circa 1950. Américo Paredes Papers, Box 12, Folder 4.

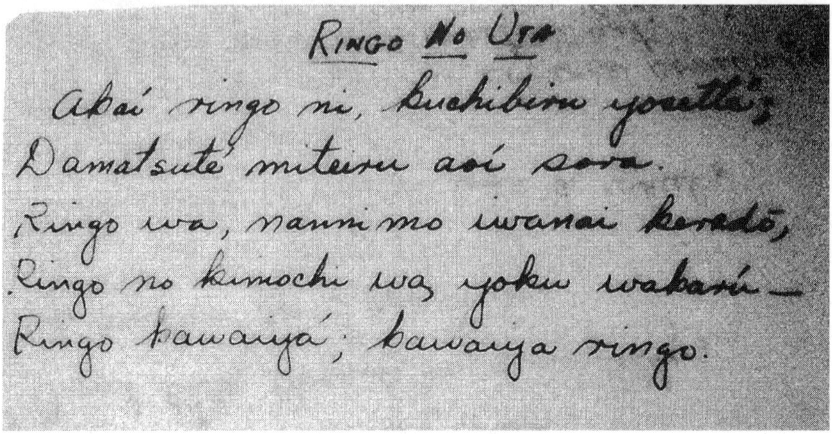

RINGO NO UTA

Akai ringo ni, kuchibiru yosetté;
Damatsuté miteiru aoi sora.
Ringo wa, nanni mo iwanai keredō,
Ringo no kimochi wa, yoku wakarú—
Ringo kawaiyá; kawaiya ringo.

Figure 52. Facsimile of handwritten lyric, "Ringo No Uta," in phonetic Japanese by Américo Paredes, circa 1950. Américo Paredes Papers, Box 12, Folder 4.

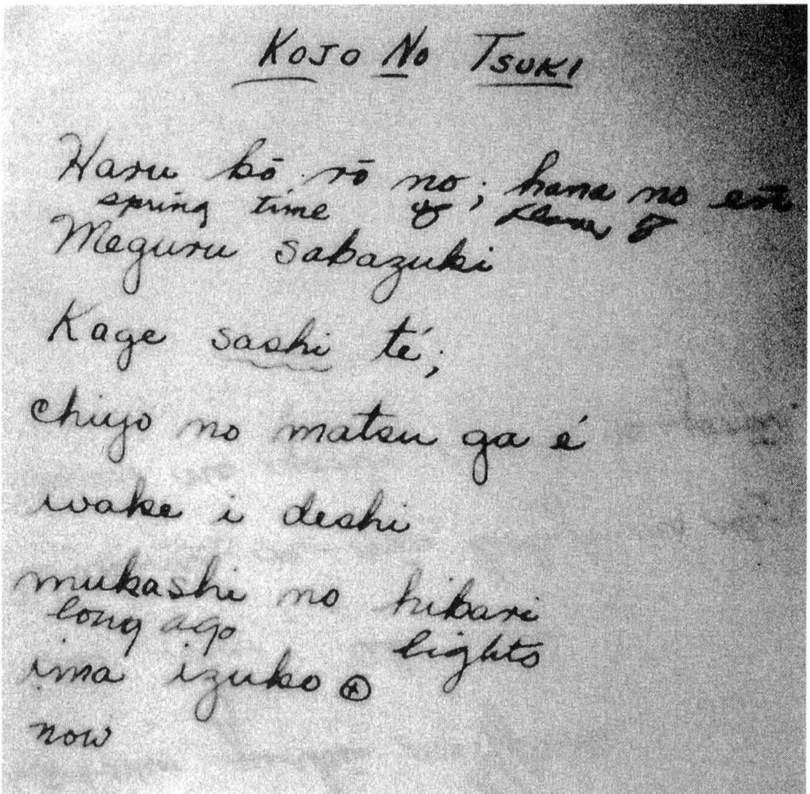

KOJO NO TSUKI

Haru kō rō no; hana no en
spring time ; flower
Meguru sabazuki
Kage sashi té;
chiyo no matsu ga é
wake i deshi
mukashi no hikari
long ago lights
ima izuko
now

Figure 53. Facsimile of handwritten lyric, "Kojo No Tsuki," in phonetic Japanese by Américo Paredes, circa 1950. Américo Paredes Papers, Box 12, Folder 4.

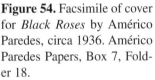

Figure 54. Facsimile of cover for *Black Roses* by Américo Paredes, circa 1936. Américo Paredes Papers, Box 7, Folder 18.

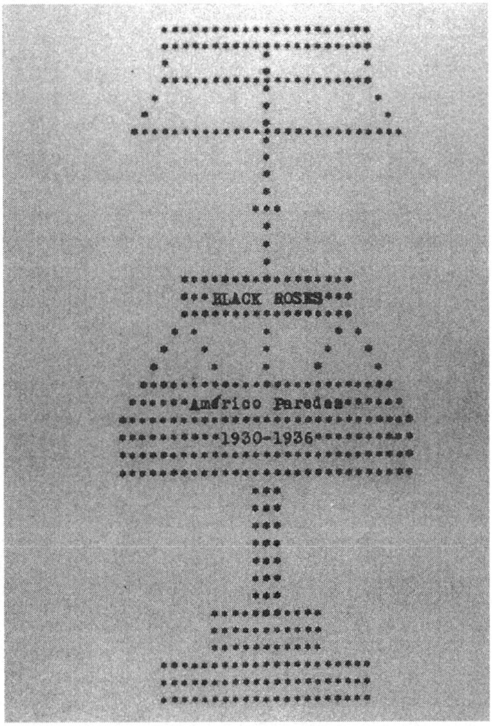

Figure 55. Facsimile of frontispiece for *Black Roses* by Américo Paredes, circa 1936. Américo Paredes Papers, Box 7, Folder 18.

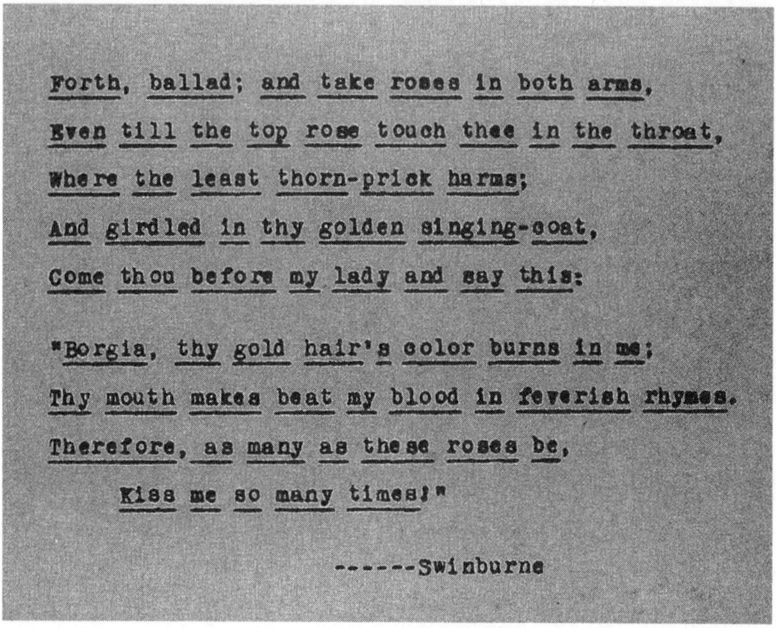

Forth, ballad; and take roses in both arms,
Even till the top rose touch thee in the throat,
Where the least thorn-prick harms;
And girdled in thy golden singing-coat,
Come thou before my lady and say this:

"Borgia, thy gold hair's color burns in me;
Thy mouth makes beat my blood in feverish rhymes.
Therefore, as many as these roses be,
Kiss me so many times!"

------Swinburne

Figure 56. Facsimile of epigraph for *Black Roses*, circa 1936. Américo Paredes Papers, Box 7, Folder 18.

Figure 57. Facsimile of illustration for *Black Roses*, circa 1936. Américo Paredes Papers, Box 7, Folder 18.

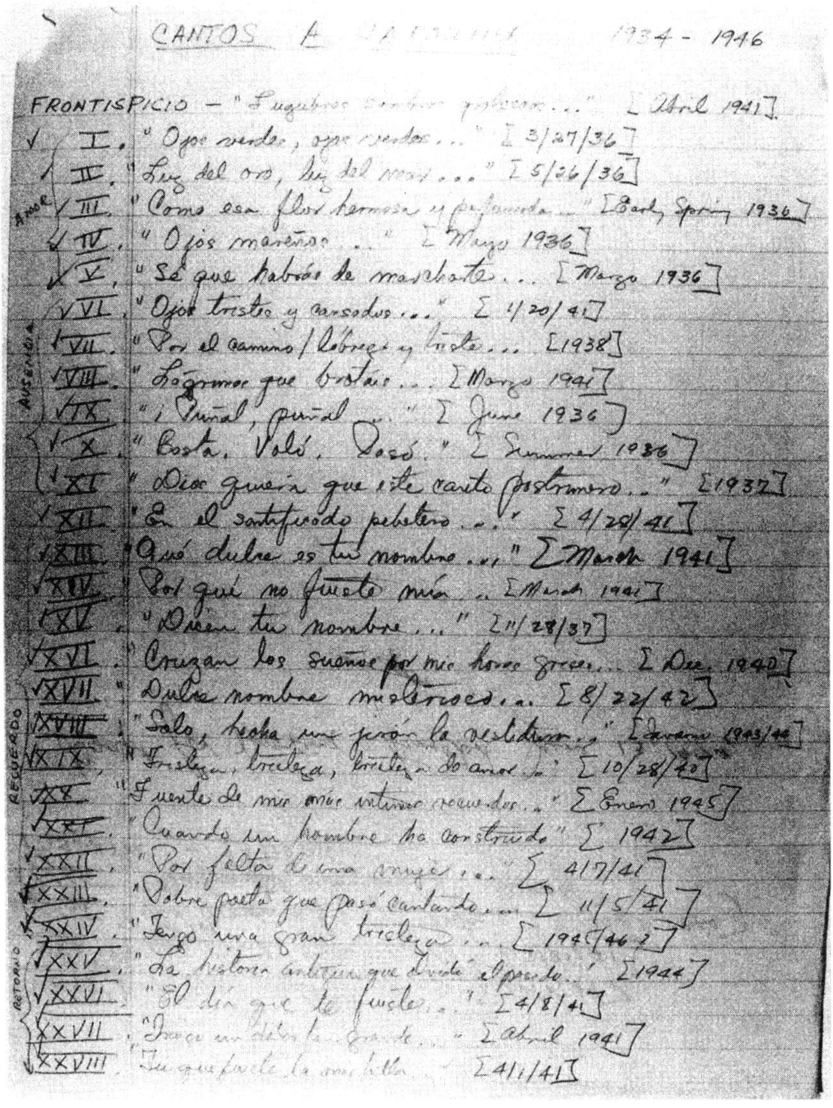

Figure 58. Facsimile of fist page in expanded table of contents for *Cantos a Carolina* (1934-1946) by Américo Paredes, date unknown. Américo Paredes Papers, Box 7, Folder 19.

Cantos de adolescencia
Songs of Youth
(1932-1937)

Prólogo

Los versos que en en este libro se encierran no son solamente el "diario de un adolescente." Son el diario de un adolescente méxico-texano.

¡Adolescente! Fenómeno físico causado por la proximidad de dos edades; individuo que no es niño ni es adulto. ¡México-texano! Fenómeno sociológico, planta de tiesto, hombre sin terruño propio y verdadero, que no es ni mexicano ni yanqui.

Los años desde 1930 hasta 1936 forman una etapa de transición en mi vida —son los años ciegos y desequilibrados de metamórfosis. Es el tiempo en que se siente la primera pasión y la primera flama del amor patrio. Es la edad en que se persiguen muchas mujeres y muchos ideales. Es el tiempo en que en el pensamiento se entabla una lucha entre la horda de ideas en embrión que allí habitan— lucha por conseguir un lugar definido y permanente en la conciencia del individuo. El niño conoció amores —pero fueron insípidos. Se sintió un momento netamente mexicano y al otro puro yanqui. Pero con la adolescencia llega el tiempo de las decisiones.

Estas páginas son el resultado de esta lucha en el tiempo de decisión. Comencé a escribir verso desde la edad de quince años pero mis obras fueron todas en inglés. Mis versos en español no comienzan hasta en 1932, dos años después. Esto se debe a la influencia de una escuela en inglés y de muy pocos libros en la lengua de Cervantes. En verdad, todavía me siento más seguro de mí mismo en la lengua de Shakespeare que en la mía. Por eso encontrará el lector en mis versos errores de gramática. Pero no crea él que están allí por falta de cuidado. La mayor parte de ellos ya fueron corregidos. Los que quedan fueron dejados al propósito, porque en mi concepto, no se pueden remover. Así —en aquellas palabras— "sentí" lo que quería decir. Decirlo de otra manera fuera no decirlo.

Mi primer verso fue a México. Desde ése hasta el último soneto se extiende esta colección ambiciosa que quise que fuera más de lo que es. Mi colección en inglés la cerré con la resolución de ya no escribir más verso en la lengua sajona.

Pero estos Cantos de adolescencia *los cierro con grandes esperanzas. Otros versos seguirán: ojalá más artísticos y más sentidos y con más conocimiento y facilidad en la lengua que llamo mía.*

Américo Paredes Manzano

Prologue[1]

The verses that are enclosed in this book are not only the "diary of an adolescent." They are the diary of a Mexico-Texan adolescent.

Adolescent! Physical phenomenon caused by the proximity of two ages; an individual who is neither a boy nor an adult. Mexico-Texan! Sociological phenomenon, potted plant, man without his own true land, who is neither Mexican nor Yankee.

The years from 1930 to 1936 form a transition stage in my life—they are the blind and unbalanced years of metamorphosis. It is the time when one experiences the first passion and the first flame of patriotic love. It is the time when one pursues many women and many ideals. It is the time when the mind sets a struggle between the herd of unborn ideas that reside there —a struggle to find a defined and permanent place in the conscience of the individual. The boy knew loves—but they were insipid. One moment he felt truly Mexican and at another purely Yankee. But with adolescence comes the time for decisions.

These pages are the result of this fight in the age of decision. I started writing verse at the age of fifteen but my works were all in English. My verses in Spanish do not begin until 1932, two years later. This is due to the influence of an English school and very few books in the language of Cervantes. In truth, I still feel more comfortable with myself in the language of Shakespeare than in my own. That is why the reader will find grammar errors in my verses. But one should not think that they are there for lack of care. The majority of them already were corrected. The ones that remain were left on purpose, because in my mind, they cannot be removed. Therefore—in those words —I "felt" what I wanted to say. To say it differently would be to not say it.

My first verse was to Mexico. From that one to the last sonnet I offer this ambitious collection, which I wish would be more than it is. I closed my English collection I closed with the resolution of never writing more verse in the Saxon language.

But I close these *Songs of Youth* with great expectations. Other verses will follow: hopefully more artistic and more heartfelt and with more knowledge and ease in the language I call my own.

Américo Paredes Manzano

La lira patriótica

The Patriotic Lyre[2]

A México

Yo te canté desde muy niño;
amor por tu suelo muy joven sentí;
mi primera poesía en nuestra lengua
fué, patria, para ti.

Yo te he visto por las páginas de historia
caída y angustiada —¡no vencida!
Has pasado por el crimen y la gloria:
heroica, sacrosanta y fratricida.

Te baña con tu sangre el insurrecto,
te vende el estadista por dinero . . .
Conozco bien, mi patria, tus defectos
y porque los conozco, yo te quiero.

Cuando sé que das un paso hacia delante
mi corazón en tierra extraña se engrandece;
y si tus hijos te hieren por la espalda,
como si a él le hirieran . . . se estremece.

. . . 3-1-36

To Mexico[3]

I sang to you since very young;
love for your land I felt as a child;
my first poetry in our own tongue
was for you, my homeland.

I've seen you through pages of history
fallen and anguished—though not defeated!
You've endured crimes and glory:
heroic, fratricidal and sacred.

The insurgent bathes you in your own blood,
for money the politician sells you . . .
I know well your flaws, my homeland,
and because I know them, I love you.

When I hear of progress that you make
my heart grows proud from foreign lands I amble;
and if your children stab you in the back,
as if my own heart were hurt . . . I tremble.

. . . 3-1-36

Himno

Canten, aves, desde árboles floridos;
canten, sauces, de cumbre hasta raíz.
Canten, ríos, alegres y movidos;
canten, vientos, que mueven el maíz.
Canten todos, en un cantar unidos,
la beldad de mi país.

Coronados sus montes de alabastro;
son sus valles bellísimo matiz.
Fue mi México el más bello diamante
en la corona de España emperatriz.
Y ahora que es libre y soberano,
más, más bello mi país.

. . . septiembre 1932

(Nota: Mi primera poesía en español.)

Hymn[4]

Sing, birds, from flowered tree;
sing, willows, from top to ground.
Sing, rivers, moving and merry;
sing, winds, that sway the cornfield.
Sing all, in a song of unity,
the beauty of my land.

Your mountains crowned with alabaster;
your valleys a beautiful shade,
my Mexico was the most beautiful diamond
in the crown empress Spain made.
And now that it is free and sovereign,
more, more beautiful is my land.

. . . September 1932

(Note: My first poem in Spanish.)

México, la ilusión del continente

Con todo respeto, al Lic. Nemesio García Naranjo. Después de escuchar su Conferencia en Matamoros, Tamps.

En tierra ajena me arrojó la vida
al sacarme del limbo de la Nada.
¿Ajena digo? ¡Tierra enajenada!
que ha tiempo fuera de mi patria herida.

Yo paso mis veinte años desgraciados
confuso en lo sajón y lo latino;
mas, pronunciando el español divino
y con los ojos en el Sur clavados.

Viendo la huella que sangrienta traza
mi pueblo, que se arroja hacia el arcano,
me he llamado sin serlo mexicano
pues he dudado de mi propia raza.

Perdido entre la duda y las querellas
he oído tu palabra palpitante
y del Infierno, como el mismo Dante
¡he salido otra vez a las estrellas!

¡Audaz tribuno de las frases bellas!
cuando la pena o el dolor me hiera,
¡enséñame a ser águila altanera
para volar contigo a las estrellas!

Y si mi espíritu se encuentra yerto,
si un César me consigna en el Calvario,
¡hazme un nopal heroico y solitario
que crece entre las peñas del desierto!

Mexico, the Illusion of the Continent[5]

With all due respect to Dr. Nemesio García Naranjo. After hearing his Presentation in Matamoros, Tamaulipas.

Life has thrown me onto foreign land
pulling me from the limbo of Oblivion.
Alien I say? Alienated station!
All this time outside my hurt homeland.

I pass my tragic twenty year youth
confused about things Latin and things English;
still, pronouncing the divine Spanish
and with eyes fixed firmly South.

Looking at the bloody footprints that trace
my people, who rush towards the arcane,
without being I have called myself Mexican
for I have doubted my own race.

Lost in doubt and in disdain
your palpitating words still engulf
and from Hell, like Dante himself,
to the stars I have come out again!

Bold herald of beautiful phrases!
When sorrow or pain wound me
teach me to be an eagle soaring free
so I can fly with you to those stars!

And if my spirit lays lifeless,
if a Ceasar consigns me to the Calvary,
make me a *nopal* heroic and solitary
that grows between desert bolder crevices!

Mi alma que en tinieblas fué indecisa
espera una palabra que la aliente;
quiere ser . . . ¡siquiera una serpiente
que hiere al presuntuoso que la pisa!

Será mi luz, la estrella que me guía
el águila, el nopal y la serpiente:
¡México! ¡La ilusión del continente!
¡México! ¡La ilusión del alma mía!

. . . 5-1-36

My soul once unsure in shadows
awaits for a word to inspire it;
I want to be . . . at least a serpent
that wounds the arrogant who tramples!

It will be my light, my guiding starshine,
the eagle, the cactus and the serpent:
Mexico! The illusion of the continent!
Mexico! The illusion of this soul of mine!

. . . 5-1-36

El sueño de Bolívar

¡De las sierras de Sonora,
del hogar del fiero Yaqui,
hijo de Mexitli el Yaqui,
hijo del feroz Mexitli,
de Mexitli, dios de guerra!

Del desierto cuyos vientos
cantan lánguidas canciones,
cantan sones de otros tiempos,
cantan en voz suave y vaga . . .
del desierto cuyos vientos
dicen —cuentan temblorosos—
de los hechos, las hazañas,
de las muertes y batallas
y del crimen y la sangre
en las tierras que atraviesan
con sus viajes incesantes.

Y que cuentan, suspirando
de amargura y de tristeza,
las leyendas amorosas,
todas llenas de misterio,
de armonía y de perfume,
de las gentes sin historia,
de los pueblos que han quedado
sobre el seno del olvido. . .

Hasta el fin del continente
que en inmensidad extiende
hacia el Sur su gran dominio
acabando en Patagonia,
donde el mismo viento vago

Bolívar's Dream[6]

From the mountains of Sonora,
from the home of the fiery Yaqui,
son of Mexitli the Yaqui,
son of the fierce Mexitli,
of Mexitli, god of war!

From the desert whose winds
sing long languid songs,
sing songs of other times,
sing in soft and wandering voice . . .
from the desert whose winds
say—tell trembling—
of deeds, of feats,
of deaths and battles
and of crime and blood
in the lands they cross
with their incessant travels.

And that tell, sighing
with bitterness and sadness,
the lovely legends,
all full of mystery,
of harmony and perfume,
of the people with no history,
of the towns that have remained
on the breast of oblivion. . .

To the end of the continent
that extends into immensity
its great dominion towards the South
ending in Patagonia,
where the same wandering wind

ya no canta ni suspira,
ya no tiembla ni solloza,
ya no llora sus recuerdos,

Sino en alas de tormenta
da tremendos alaridos,
¡grita el grito de la guerra
contra todo lo que vive!

Este inmenso territorio
que en su tiempo ha conocido
a los incas y toltecas,
los aztecas y los mayas
y más tarde ha despertado
con el paso conquistante
de Cortés y de Pizarro
es la América Latina,
es la tierra del futuro,
es la patria de Bolívar.

¡O Bolívar! ¡o coloso!
¡o guerrero apasionado!
¿Fué tan alto, puro y vano
aquel sueño que soñaste?

Fué tan alto como el vuelo
del cóndor sobre los Andes,
del cóndor, rey de las aves,
compañero de las nubes,
que contempla solitario
desde su serena altura
la avaricia y la lujuria
de este mundo de los hombres.

no longer sings nor sighs,
no longer trembles nor wails,
no longer cries its memories,

Rather in wings of a storm
makes tremendous howls,
shouts the cry of war
against all that lives!

This immense territory
that in its time has known
the Incas and Toltecs,
the Aztecs and the Mayas
and later has awakened
with the conquering march
of Cortés and Pizarro
it is Latin America,
it is the land of the future,
it is the land of Bolívar.

O Bolívar! O colossus!
O impassioned warrior!
Was it so exalted, pure and vain
that dream you dreamed?

It was as high as the flight
of the condor over the Andes,
of the condor, king of the birds,
companion of clouds,
that contemplates alone
from its serene height
the avarice and greed
of this world of men.

Fue tan puro como nieve
que la tierra no ha tocado,
como gota de rocío
en un cáliz de amapola,
¡lágrima que la alborada
vió en los ojos de la noche!

¿Vano? ¿Porque tú caíste
sin que fuera realizado?
¿y por eso fué miraje
que seduce al caminante?
¿y por eso fué la espuma
de los mares que tú araste?

No ha caído en tierra infértil
la semilla que sembraste
y que regada está con sangre;
lo que echaste tú a los mares
sobre las inquietas aguas
llegará a la playa un día.

. . . primavera 1934

It was as pure as snow
that the earth has not touched,
like a drop of dew
in the chalice of a poppy,
tear that the woodlands
saw in the eyes of night!

Vain? Because you fell
without it being realized?
And for this it was a mirage
that seduces the traveler?
And for this the foam
of the oceans you plowed?

It has not fallen on infertile land
the seed you sowed
and watered well with blood;
what you threw into the seas
over restless waters
will arrive on the beach one day.

. . . Spring 1934

La música

Music

Guadalupe la Chinaca

a Blanca Reducinda

¿Qué tiene esa voz tan lastimera
que en sus lamentos

lleva lo agridulce de la sierra—
aquellos melancólicos acentos
de canción ranchera?

¿De quién es la canción que así se queja
dolorida?

Parece ser el canto de mi vieja
patria herida.

Canta, Guadalupe la Chinaca,
canta, canta;

deja que el zenzontli herido llore
en tu garganta;

canta tu canción "remexicana"
porque al cantarla

entre sus quejas sollozantes
¡México me habla!

Llevas en tu canto la frescura
de aires costeños,

todos los secretos y dulzura
de mis ensueños,

Guadalupe la Chinaca[7]

To Blanca Reducinda

What's in that voice so tragic
        its laments

carry the bittersweet of mountains—
        those melancholic accents
        of *ranchera* music?

Whose is the song that complains
        so pained?

It must to be the song of my old
        wounded motherland.

Sing, *Guadalupe la Chinaca*,
        sing, sing;

Let the wounded *zenzontli* cry
        in your throat;

Sing that *Mexican* song
        because by singing

through its sobbing complaints
        Mexico speaks to me!

You carry in your song the freshness
        of coastal airs,

all the secrets and sweetness
        of my desires,

lánguidos susurros soñadores
de platanales,

todo el aroma de las flores
primaverales,

todo el hechizo de tu tierra,
tierra caliente,

toda la queja de la sierra,
queja doliente,

cántico del rústico galante,
notas tan llenas

de todo el anhelo palpitante
de las morenas.

Canta, que La Voz de los violines
cual sangre mana,

Y la guitarra en ricas perlas
se desgrana.

Canta, Guadalupe la Chinaca,
canta, canta;

deja que el zenzontli herido llore
en tu garganta;

canta tu canción "remexicana"
porque al cantarla

entre sus quejas sollozantes
¡México me habla!

. . . 6-7-36

languid dreamy whispers
of banana orchards,

all the aromas
of springtime flowers

all the magic of your land,
hot land,

all the mountain cries,
painful cries,

gospel of the rustic gallant
notes so full

with all the palpitating want
of dark women.

Sing, that the voice of violins
flows like blood,

And the guitar of rich pearls
releases its jewels.

Sing, *Guadalupe la Chinaca*,
sing, sing;

let the wounded *zenzontli* cry
in your throat;
sing that *Mexican* song
because by singing

through its sobbing complaints
Mexico speaks to me!

. . . 6-7-36

Canciones

La guitarra llora;
la guitarra canta.
Lamenta el violín . . .

¡Y una voz impetuosa
—con el alma en su canto—
sencilla y serrana,
con ardor se levanta
en la música hermosa
de canción mexicana!

Qué tendrán tus canciones, patria mía;
qué tendrán tus canciones.
Que gritan con salvaje lozanía,
que lloran como tristes corazones.

Qué tendrán tus corridos, tus huapangos,
tus tristes yucatecas y tus sones.
Qué tendrán tus canciones, patria mía;
¡qué tendrán tus canciones!

. . . abril 1935

Songs[8]

The guitar cries;
the guitar sings.
The violin laments . . .

And an impetuous voice—
with the soul in its song—
simple and mountainous,
with ardor it arises,
in the beautiful sounds
of Mexican song!

What's in your songs, homeland of mine;
what's in your songs.
That scream with wild pride,
that cry like sad hearts.

What's in your *corridos*, your *huapangos*,
your sad *yucatecas* and your *sones*.
What's in your songs, homeland of mine;
What's in your songs!

. . . *April 1935*

Paso doble

Ah, fiera y palpitante melodía,
grito de mujer-pantera bruna,
aire que en Granada tuvo cuna
y madre en la pasión de Andalucía.

Espíritu indomable, alma bravía,
alma entristecida de gitana,
cuerpo de sensual diosa pagana
—¡derroche de hermosura y lozanía!

Encierra aquel orgullo de la España
que supo despachar a tierra extraña
lo mejor de su sangre brava y noble.

Encierra la arrogancia y gallardía
y todo aquel desdén de la hidalguía
el ritmo arrobador de un paso doble.

. . . 1-16-34

Paso Doble[9]

Oh, fierce and throbbing melodies,
shout of brown panther woman,
a wind from Granada you were born
and mother the passion of Andaluz skies.

Untamed spirit, soul courageous,
a gypsy soul sad and down,
a god's body sensuous and pagan—
beauty and pride in total excess!

You enshrine that pride of Spain
that brilliantly sent to lands foreign
the best of its brave and noble blood.

You enshrine arrogance and gallantry
and all that disdain of nobility
the enraptured rhythm of a *paso doble*.

. . . 1-16-34

Rumba

Lejos de mí los suaves madrigales,
los pájaros de voces lastimeras;
quiero en mi oído el grito de las fieras,
quiero sentir pasiones animales

que escondidas en duros matorrales
de la mente, esperaban cual panteras
—sensuales cual meneo de caderas
en éxtasis de bailes bacanales.

¡Ah, canto que con tu fiereza dueles!
del África naciste, rumba ardiente,
y tienes un sabor de hierro y hieles.

Canción espiritual nunca se siente;
lo místico, lo triste, tiene mieles
—¡lo carnal, lo salvaje, es aguardiente!

. . . 6-20-34

Rumba[10]

So distant the soft madrigals,
birds with voices so sad and mild;
I want to hear the shout of the wild,
I want to feel animal passions

hidden in thicket branches
of the mind, like panthers waiting—
sensuous like a hip swing
in ecstasy of Bachannalian dances.

Oh, song who hurts with ferocity!
Burning rumba, from Africa you have dwelled,
and you taste of iron and hostility.

Spiritual song is never felt;
the mystical, the tragic, still has beauty
the carnal, the savage, an intoxicant!

. . . 6-20-34

La naturaleza
Nature

Oración

¡Beldad exótica! ¡Princesa mora!
¡ah, Noche! ¡triste Diosa! ¡Madre mía!
hermana de la Muerte obscura y fría,
¡escucha mi alma débil que te implora!

Tiende doquier tu sombra bienhechora
que ya el bullicio y el calor del día
claváronme sus garras de porfía,
¡ah, ven, dulcísima, que mi alma llora!

No busco a tu hijo el de las alas bellas
—al Sueño no lo espero. Ah, Sultana,
más grande es el deleite de mirarte.

Ven, tú, con el turbante hecho de estrellas
y en tu frente la luna musulmana,
¡que quiero en las tinieblas adorarte!

. . . 7-15-36

Prayer[11]

Exotic beauty! Moorish princess!
Oh, Night! Sad Goddess! Mother of me!
Sister of Death cold and dreary,
listen to my weak soul that implores!

Spread out your shadow of goodness,
for the racket and warmth of the day
have nailed me with their stubborn claws already!
Oh, come, sweet thing, for my soul cries!

I do not seek your son of pretty wings—
I do not await Sleep. Oh, Sultanness,
much greater is the delight of seeing you.

Come, you, with turban made of starlings
and the Muslim moon upon your face,
for in the darkness I want to worship you.

. . . 7-15-36

El Río Bravo

Río Bravo, Río Bravo,
que en tu cauce lento vas
con frecuentes remolinos,
cual si quieres ir atrás.

cual si quieren tus corrientes
sobre el cauce devolver
a buscar ignotas fuentes
que les dieron vida y ser,

así vas —mientras tus aguas
lloran, lloran sin cesar—
a morirte lentamente
a las márgenes del mar.

Mis pasiones y mis cuitas
en tu seno quiero ahogar;
llévate el dolor de mi alma
en tu parda inmensidad.

Que he nacido a tus orillas
y muy joven ya sentí
que hay en mi alma torbellinos,
que ella se parece a ti.

Turbia, sí, de fondo obscuro,
mas el Sol le hace brillar;
con suspiros —rebeliones—
y bregando sin cesar.

The Rio Grande[12]

Muddy river, muddy river,
Moving slowly down your track
With your swirls and counter-currents,
As though wanting to turn back,

As though wanting to turn back
Towards the place where you were born,
While your currents swirl and eddy,
While you whisper, whimper, and mourn;

So you wander down your channel
Always on, since it must be,
Till you die so very gently
By the margin of the sea.

All my pain and all my trouble
In your bosom let me hide,
Drain my soul of all its sorrow
As you drain the countryside,

For I was born beside your waters,
And since very young I knew
That my soul had hidden currents,
That my soul resembled you,

Troubled, dark, its bottom hidden
While its surface mocks the sun,
With its sighs and its rebellions,
Yet compelled to travel on.

Cuando muera, cuando muera
y se pudra el cuerpo ya,
mi alma, como riachuelo
a tus aguas correrá.

Pasaremos por los campos
que se mirarán verdear,
por jacales de rancheros,
a las ruinas de Bagdad . . . .

Y tus aguas moribundas
en lo azul se perderán,
mientras duermo dulcemente
a las márgenes del mar.

. . . 7-21-36

When the soul must leave the body,
When the wasted flesh must die,
I shall trickle forth to join you,
In your bosom I shall lie;

We shall wander through the country
Where your banks in green are clad,
Past the shanties of rancheros,
By the ruins of old Baghdad,

Till at last your dying waters,
Will release their hold on me,
and my soul will sleep forever
By the margin of the sea.

. . . 7-21-36

El huracán

Del mar se acerca con gigantes pasos,
del mar, que siendo inmune, le enfurece;
la brisa, débil hembra, enmudece
cuando en el norte ve sus negros trazos.

Ya se oye su rugido que amenaza;
se ve el relampagear de sus pupilas
que anuncian destrucción, cual dos Atilas . . .
¡Se siente lo pesado de su maza!

Se agitan sus vestidos harapientos;
resuena por los cielos su alarido;
y cae sobre ciudad y sobre ejido
¡la furia del guerrero de los vientos!

. . . 7-24-34

The Hurricane[13]

From sea with great steps it approaches,
from the sea, so free, it enrages him;
and the wind, weak little girl, just goes dim
when up north she sees its dark black traces.

And now its ominous rumble is heard;
you can see the lightning of its pupils
that announce destruction, like two Attilas . . .
You can feel the weight of its mace hard!

Its dirty ragged clothes stir;
over the skies its holler resounds;
and on city and farm descends
the fury of the wind warrior!

. . . 7-24-34

Primavera en la ciudad

Estoy aprisionado entre mansiones,
por fincas imponentes rodeado,
las nuevas levantando sus bastiones
más alto que han las otras alcanzado;
van hacia arriba en avaricia y celo
como gigantes en feroz combate . . .

¡Quiero estar en el campo al libre cielo!
donde el Bravo enverdece sus riberas,
donde hay siempre primavera ¡y hay rancheras
de ojos verdes y labios de granate!

. . . invierno 1932

Spring in the City[14]

I am imprisoned among mansions,
by impressive estates besieged,
new ones raising their bastions
higher than the others have reached;
they reach up with avarice and jealous
like giants in ferocious combat. . .

I want to be in open air of the country!
where the Rio Grande greens its shores,
where there is always spring and ranchgirls
with green eyes and lips garnet and rosy!

. . . Winter 1932

Tarde de otoño

Con quejumbrosa voz, el triste viento
que gime sollozante mis dolores
azota sin piedad las negras flores
que tiene mi jardín del pensamiento.

Entonces el espíritu sediento,
que ahogado por pasiones y rencores
callaba su desdicha y sus temores,
se queja de la vida en canto lento.

La tarde, la magnífica pintura
que traza el Astro-Rey al fin del día,
el viento que se queja y que murmura

y la llegada de la noche fría
alejan poco a poco la amargura
y traen consigo la melancolía.

. . . septiembre 1933

Autumn's Evening[15]

With a quivering voice, the distraught wind
that hollers and sobs my tortures
mercilously beats the black flowers
that the garden of my thought contained.

Then the thirsty spirit, so drowned
with deep passions and angers
it silenced its misery and fears,
about life in a low chant complained.

The evening, a magnificent painting
that traces the Star-King at the end of the day,
the wind that complains murmuring

and the night so icy arriving
little by little discard the bitterness away
and with them melancholy they bring.

. . . September 1933

Serenata de plata

Luna que serena brillas,
blanca reina majestuosa,
casta Diana, bella diosa,
dueña de las serranías
donde con tus manos frías
mueves el pincel plateado,
transformando todo el prado
en caprichosas fantasías,
luna, ¡qué serena brillas!

Plata el campo, el río plata,
plata el sauce rociado
que susurra y que se acata . . .
¡La guitarra se desata!
¡Un galante plateado
canta blanca serenata!

. . . invierno 1932

Silver Serenade[16]

Moon who shines so serene,
a white queen of majesty,
chaste Diana, goddess of beauty,
monarch of all the mountain
where with a cold handed design
you move the silvered pen holy,
transforming the meadow holly
into whimsical fantasy green,
moon, how you shine so serene!

Silver the field, the silver river,
silver the dew-filled willow
that obeys with its whisper . . .
The guitar rattles its hollow!
A silver clad courtier
sings a serenade of snow!

. . . Winter 1932

Noche

¡Noche!
Diosa que viste nacer al universo,
reina absoluta de lo que más allá se extiende,
¡Noche! ¡Negra flor!

De lo más tenebroso de tus entrañas
mi alma levanta una queja,
un gemido al infinito,
una queja
de angustia, de soledad —del indecible deseo.
Cuando reinas suprema sobre el mundo soñoliento.
con las estrellas entre tus cabellos
y la luna en tu frente morena,
suenan en mis oídos las notas
de tu música silenciosa . . .
Y la parte de ti que en mí se aloja
anhela desesperadamente por desprenderse
de la tierra,
por volar hacia arriba
a mezclarse,
a confundirse,
a hacerse una con tu inmensidad.
¡Noche! ¡Negra flor!

. . . primavera 1933

Night[17]

Night!
Goddess who saw the universe born,
true queen of what extends beyond,
Night! Black flower!

From the darkest depths of your entrails
my soul raises a complaint,
a moan into infinity
a complaint
of anguish, loneliness—of the unspeakable desire.
When you reign supreme over the slumbering world,
with the stars between your hairs
and the moon on your brown face,
the notes of your silent music
resound in my ears . . .
And the piece of you residing in me
desperately longs to break free
from the earth,
to fly upwards
to mix itself,
to confuse itself,
to make itself one with your immensity.
Night! Black flower!

. . . Spring 1933

La comedia del amor

The Comedy of Love

Canción

Tú eres la causa que yo me encuentre
sobre los mares de poesía
y si mi barca naufragaría
yo me ahogaría en ridiculez.

Tú eres la causa que yo me encuentre
diciendo cosas que no debía
Mas, si tu orgullo lo permitiera
¡qué me dijera tu alma a la vez!

. . . agosto 1933

Song[18]

You have pushed me to the brink
of the seas of poetry,
and if my ship should sink
I would drown in absurdity.

You have pushed me to the brink
of saying things that should not be.
But, if your pride would think
oh, what your soul would say to me!

. . . August 1933

No sias creido

No sias creido, Pantalión;
son iguales las mujeres
y por más que tú las queres,
son traidoras, Pantalión.

Te dicen —Por ti 'stoy loca;
eres 'lúnico, mi amor . . .
y te dejan por otro siñor
abriendo tamaña boca.

Con tu probe corazón
nomás queren jugar un rato.
¡No sias bruto! ¡No sias bruto!
¡No sias creido, Pantalión!

. . . 10-29-35

Don' Be Conceited[19]

Don' be conceited Pantaloon;
all women are the same
even tho' you luv 'em,
they betray, Pantaloon.

They say—I'm crazy for you;
you're th' only one, love of mine . . .
then leave you for another man
mouth wide as they do.

With your po' heart's swoon
they only wanna play a while.
Don' be stupid! Don' be a fool!
Don' be conceited, Pantaloon!

. . . *10-29-35*

A una sajona

Si te dijera: Tu mirada triste
le dio un feliz instante a mi existencia;
tus ojos que reflejan la inocencia,
con ellos —¡yo no sé lo que me hiciste!

Si te dijera: Cuando sonreíste
mataste la razón y la experiencia
en mí, ¡tus labios tienen tal potencia!
¿Dirías lo que en sueños me dijiste?

Si te dijera —¡pero no te digo!
Ya supe lo que son tus ojos güeros
que buscan nada más jugar conmigo.

Ojos tristes son siempre traicioneros
y aunque me llene de pasión contigo,
conozco ya tus viejos correderos.

. . . 7-30-34

To An Anglo Girl[20]

If I were to say: Your gaze of melancholy
brought some joy to my existence;
your eyes that mirror innocence,
with them—I don't know what you did to me!

If I were to say: When you smiled gaily
you murdered my reason and experience,
your lips have that omnipotence!
Would you say what in dreams you spoke to me?

If I were to say—but I don't say!
I already knew the truth about your pale eyes
that want nothing more but to play.

Sad eyes always betray
and though you fill me with desires
I already know well your old way.

. . . 7-30-34

Fábula

Una ninfa nació entre los cisneros;
le tocó ser tan grácil y tan bella
que parecía solitaria estrella
en los pálidos cielos mañaneros.

Oyeme, tú, serena y casta luna,
tú gozaste al brillar en sus ojazos;
¡la viste juguetear entre lampazos
con los cisnes de nieve en la laguna!

Y los faunos y sátiros ardientes
buscaban anhelantes sus amores;
más a todos la ninfa daba flores
y se reía de sus pretendientes.

Y de todos la ninfa se burlaba
mas encontróse un día junto al río
a un pensativo sátiro sombrío
que ni alzaba el mirar ni la buscaba.

Enfadóse la bella a esos desdenes;
poniéndose también muy desdeñosa
al sátiro le dijo muy airosa:
—¡Habla! ¿Quién eres tú? ¿De dónde vienes?

Y él contestó: —Soy bardo peregrino;
vengo de ignotas y áridas regiones;
no traigo más que el polvo del camino
y nada sé mas que cantar canciones.

Sí, mucho polvo, sí; que eres reseco
—la ninfa respondió en alegre chanza.

Fable[21]

A nymph was born among swan tides;
it was so beautiful and slender
she seemed like a lonely star
in the pale morning skies.

Hear me, you, calm and chaste moon,
you enjoyed shinning in her eyes bright;
saw her play in the pastoral height
with swans of snow in the lagoon!

And the fawns and burning satyrs
searched longing for her loves;
but to all, the nymph gave cloves
and just laughed at all her suitors.

And the nymph ridiculed them all.
until she found by the river
a sad and pensive satyr
who took no notice nor did call.

Our beauty grew mad at that disdain;
and also gave a disdainful look
and to the satyr angrily spoke:
—Speak! Who are you? What is your origin.

And he replied: I am a wandering bard;
I come from dry and unknown lands;
I have nothing but the dust of the road
and know only how to sing my chants.

Yes, too much dust, yes; you are dried out—
the nymph replied with a happy phrase.

Vamos a ver, Orfeo, una alabanza
a mi hermosura; ¡que resuene el eco!
Tañó el laúd con mano exploradora,
dando a la ninfa una mirada fría;
¡cual brota el llanto de mujer que llora
del poeta brotó la melodía!. . .

Mariposa, mariposa,
mariposa de alegres galas,
cuídate bien las alas,
mariposa, mariposa.
Bella rosa, bella rosa,
rosa que me perfuma;
la hermosura es una espuma,
bella, bella, bella rosa.

Posa el pensamiento, posa
la mirada en el futuro;
cae el fruto ya maduro
y en el suelo se destroza.
Mariposa, mariposa,
mariposa de alegres galas,
cuídate bien las alas,
mariposa, mariposa.

Y al oírme cantar de esta manera,
te fuiste, altiva náyade, te fuiste;
te marchaste muy bella y altanera
mas, a pesar de todo . . . un poco triste.

. . . 7-26-36

Let us see, Orpheus, a praise
to my beauty; let the echo shout!

He played the lute with wandering hand,
giving the nymph a cold stare;
like tears springing from a weeping woman
the poet let loose a melodious air!. . .

Butterfly, butterfly,
butterfly of lively dress,
watch well your wing tress,
butterfly, butterfly.
Beautiful rose, beautiful rose,
rose that perfumes my nose;
this beauty is a mist that grows,
beautiful, beautiful, beautiful rose.

Lay your mind, lay
your sight on the future;
the fruit will drop when mature
and on the ground it will die.
Butterfly, butterfly,
butterfly of lively dress,
watch well your wing tress,
butterfly, butterfly.

And when you heard me sing it so
you left, you left, proud nyad;
pretty and proud you did go
and, in spite of it all . . . a little sad.

. . . 7-26-36

Amor y rosas

Una rosa tú me diste,
una bella, roja flor,
y pregunta tú me hiciste:
"Dime, ¿qué se llama amor?"

Si pudiera yo saber
cuantas mariposas
vienen a beber
del néctar de tus rosas,
pudiera yo, mujer,
explicarte tales cosas.

Más . . . es como las rosas
la pasión llamada amor:
un momento sonrosada,
cual la rosa que me diste,
para mañana triste
y pasado deshojada.

Como flor,
como flor que tú me diste,
es tan frágil y tan triste
lo que se le llama amor.

. . . 10-29-35

Love and Roses[22]

A rose you gave,
a beautiful, red rose,
and the question you pose:
"Tell me: What is love?"

If I could know
how many butterflies
come to swallow
the nectar of your roses,
woman, I could go
explain to you all this.

For . . . it is like roses
the passion called love:
for a moment it blushes,
like the rose you gave,
by tomorrow sad gushes
and a day later not a leaf.

Like a rose,
like a rose you gave,
so fragil and full of woes
that which is called love.

. . . 10-29-35

Juguete (I)

Entre fragantes y lucientes flores,
más bella que la pálida azucena,
yo te contemplo, angelical morena,
¡sultana del harén de mis amores!

Llorando sin voz por mis dolores
en el jardín sin fin de tu recuerdo
volviendo a recordarte así me pierdo
entre fragantes y lucientes flores.

Recuerdo tu faz de virgen nazarena,
tu boca de coral, tus ojos vivos,
expresión de tu raza, hispano-altivos
más bella que la pálida azucena.

Hiere mi corazón la fiera pena;
pero aún recuerdo tu figura esbelta
y con el alma en la ilusión envuelta,
yo te contemplo, angelical morena.

Y por siempre en el jardín de mis dolores
cortaré de azucenas exquisitas,
las flores de ayer, flores marchitas
¡sultana del harén de mis amores!

. . . 4-30-36

(Nota: Las primeras cuatro líneas de Roberto Ramírez, así como la última de las otras estancias. Las demás en tipo negro de Sabás Klahn; las restantes de Paredes.)

Toy (I)[23]

Between brilliant and fragrant flowers,
more beautiful than a white lilly's pale,
I adore you, beautiful brown angel,
sultanness from the harem of my lovers.

Crying in silence from my sorrows
in the endless garden of your memory,
with each thought I lose my way
between brilliant and fragrant flowers.

I remember your Nazarene face virginal,
your coral mouth, you lively eyes,
Hispanic-proud, symbol of your race,
more beautiful than a white lilly's pale.

My heart hurts infernal;
but I still remember your slender disposition
and with my soul caught in the illusion,
I adore you, beautiful brown angel.

And forever in the garden of my sorrows
I will cut from exquisite lillies,
the flowers of yesterday, withered flowers
sultanness from the harem of my lovers!

. . . 4-30-36

(Note: The first four lines are from Roberto Ramírez, as are the last of the other stanzas. The others in bold [italics here] are from Sabás Klahn; the rest from Paredes.)

Juguete (II)

Mi vida es una rosa deshojada;
cada pétalo es una ilusión.
Mi vida es una rosa destrozada
por el tiempo, la vida y la pasión.

Llegó al jardín de mi temprana vida
el duro cierzo con su mano helada,
dejando mi ilusión así esparcida:
mi vida es una rosa deshojada.

Llegó la ráfaga del cruel invierno
y destrozó mi flor del corazón;
perdió sus pétalos al hondo cieno:
cada pétalo es una ilusión.

Ya ni el perfume de la rosa queda,
sólo el recuerdo de la infiel amada
como un solo pétalo que rueda
mi vida es una rosa destrozada.

Y en horas tristes cuando sola el alma
musita a solas con su decepción,
comprende y llora —que perdió la calma
por el tiempo, la vida y la pasión.

. . . 4-30-36

(Nota: Las primeras dos líneas de Ramírez, las segundas dos de Paredes. Las otras nuevas: de Klahn las de tipo negro y de Paredes las demás.)

Toy (II)[24]

My life is a rose withered;
each petal an illusion.
My life is a rose ruined
by time, life and pasion.

To the garden of my young life came
the harsh north wind's frozen hand,
leaving my illusion scattered lame:
my life is a rose withered.

The blast of cruel winter arrived
and tore the flower of my affection;
it lost its petals in the deep mud:
each petal is an illusion.

Now not even the rose's perfume remains
only the memory of the unfaithful beloved
like a single petal that tumbles
my life is a rose ruined.

And in sad hours when the soul is alone
it mumbles lonely with its deception,
it understands and cries—all calm gone
by time, life and passion.

. . . 4-30-36

(Note: The first two lines are from Ramírez, the second ones from Paredes. The other new ones: from Klahn in bold [italics here] and from Paredes the rest.)

Lágrimas negras

Llora el mar y sus arenas
lo que yo estoy padeciendo;
llora la pluma escribiendo
*negras lágrimas de penas.**

Vago estas playas ajenas
cabizbajo y pensativo
y viendo el dolor en que vivo,
llora el mar y sus arenas.

Eres rosa y rosa siendo
con tu aroma ideal me inspiras
—tú que ni sabes ni miras
lo que yo estoy padeciendo.

Vago mis penas diciendo
por ti, amor de mis amores,
y viendo mis sinsabores
llora la pluma escribiendo.

Y viendo que me encadenas
con tus manos exquisitas,
brotan del alma marchitas
¡negras lágrimas de penas!

. . . 4-30-36

*(Nota: de don Justo Cisneros, bisabuelo del que escribe.)

Black Tears[25]

Sea and sands grieve
what I am suffering;
the pen writes crying
black tears of grief.*

I wander these foreign reefs
crestfallen and pensive
and seeing the pain I live,
sea and sands grieve.

You are a rose and rose being
your perfect aroma inspires me—
you who cannot know or see
what I am suffering.

I wander my sorrows saying
for you, love of my love,
and seeing me grieve
the pen writes crying.

And being chained without relief
by your exquisite hand,
from my soul bursts withered
black tears of grief!

. . . 4-30-36

**(Note: By Don Justo Cisneros, great grandfather of the writer.)*

Ojos tristes

Ojos tristes, ojos tristes,
dulze imagen que he soñado,
ay de mí, de mí cuitado,
mira el dolo que ficiste.

Corasón, todo le distes,
nunca quísote ella, nunca,
con el alma trunca, trunca,
de su vida tú te fuistes.

Ojos tristes, ojos tristes,
bello ser idolatrado,
ay de mí, de mí cuitado,
mira el mal que me ficistes.

. . . 7-8-36

Sad Eyes[26]

Sad eyes, sad eyes,
sweet image I have dreamt,
woe is me, my lament,
see the pain you devise.

Heart, you gave her all,
never did she love you back, never,
with severed soul, severed,
out of her life you did fall.

Sad eyes, sad eyes,
good to be worshipped,
woe is me, my lament,
see the wrong you did devise.

. . . 7-8-36

Serenata

Luna que sabes mi mal,
luna que ves mi dolor,
vé a la ventana a mirar
si duerme mi amor . . .
duerme mi amor.

Estrellas que encienden al mar
cirios de incierto fulgor,
vengan también a velar
que duerme mi amor . . .
duerme mi amor.

Brisa del amanecer,
besa sus labios de flor
—céfiro quisiera ser . . .
y duerme mi amor . . .
duerme mi amor.

. . . invierno 1932

Serenade[27]

Moon who knows what ails me,
moon who sees my pain,
go to the window and see
if my love sleeps . . .
my love sleeps.

Stars that light the sea
candles of unknown splendor,
also come watch and see
because my love sleeps . . .
my love sleeps.

Sunrise breeze, sunrise breeze,
kiss her flowered lips—
zephyr I wish to be . . .
and my love sleeps . . .
my love sleeps.

. . . Winter 1932

Si tú supieras

Si tú supieras lo que sufre el alma
cuando por otra llora silenciosa,
si tú supieras, joven caprichosa,
si tú supieras lo que duele el alma . . .

Si tú supieras lo que duele el alma
y si en la tuya sintieras el anhelo,
si conocieras el cruel desdén y el celo,
muy bien supieras lo que sufre el alma.

Si conocieras la dicha atormentada
que causa con mirar un ser querido,
si tú tuvieras el corazón herido,
si tú estuvieras realmente enamorada,

y si tuvieras el alma dolorida
a causa de un amor sincero y puro,
bebieras, vida mía, te lo juro,
del néctar que Cupido nos convida.

Y si supieras lo corto que es la vida,
si tú supieras, criatura de una hora,
que por más bella y rosada que es la aurora
muy pronto quedará desvanecida,

si tú supieras que cada flor que nace
en poco tiempo queda deshojada,
que de los hombres quedará olvidada
cuando su bello rojo se deshace . . .

If You Knew[28]

If you knew what the soul suffers
when it silently cries for another,
if you knew, capricios lover,
if you knew what the soul endures.

If you knew what the soul endures
and if in your own you felt the yearning,
if you knew jealousy and cruel disdaining,
you would know well how the soul suffers.

If you felt that tormented love
that comes from seeing a beloved,
if you had your heart wounded,
if you truly were in love,

and if you had your soul aching
from a love sincere and pure,
you would drink, my love, I assure,
from the nectar of Cupid's offering.

And if you knew how life goes by,
if you knew, my sweet little thing,
that however pretty and pink the morning
soon enough it will fade away,

if you knew that each birthing flower
in little time will defoliate,
that from men's minds it will disintegrate
when its lovely red goes sour . . .

Muy pronto dejarías de tu impío
jugar con corazones —¡amarías!
y un par de copas llenas me darías
del vino que el futuro haría mío.

¡Bah! Yo no soy ansioso de licores,
son altos y divinos mis antojos;
las copas que yo quiero son tus ojos . . .
pues bríndame con ellos tus amores.

¡Ah, Tiempo que nos guías caminante
por sendas espinosas y sin tregua!
Los hombres llaman año a cada legua
que andamos en la marcha incesante . . .

La yungla del pasado traicionero
esconde a cuatro leguas la tableta
en cual un día quiso tu poeta
grabar en letras de oro: YO TE QUIERO.

. . . verano 1933

Very soon you would quit your profane
play with hearts—you would love!
and a pair of filled cups you would give
with wine that time would make mine.

Bah! I am not anxious for liquors
my cravings are noble and higher;
your eyes are the glasses I desire . . .
so with them give that love of yours.

Oh! Time who guides us on
through thorny paths without falter!
Men call a year each league they saunter
in our ceaseless marathon . . .

The jungle of the evil milieu
four leagues in hides the tablet
in which one day decided your poet
to engrave in gold letters: I LOVE YOU.

. . . *Summer 1933*

Rima (I)

Hay unos ojos que si me miran
hacen que llore mi corazón;
hay unos labios que si suspiran
me parten l'alma sin compasión.

Ah, labios vivos; ay, labios rojos,
¿por qué suspiran? —¿por qué arrebatan?
ay, ojos tristes; ay, lindos ojos,
¿por qué me miran? ¿por qué me matan?

Hay unas manos, diáfanas manos,
color de nieve cual blanco tul;
hay unos brazos esculturales
con entre-encajes de leve azul.

Ay, ojos tristes, lindos ojazos,
ay, vivos labios de carmesí,
ay, blancas manos; ay, bellos brazos,
en vuestros lazos,
en vuestros lazos quiero morir.

. . . 5-8-36

Rhyme (I)[29]

There are eyes whose gaze
would cause my heart to cry;
there are lips whose simple sigh
would rip my soul with craze.

Oh, lively lips; oh, red lips,
why do you sigh?—why do you thrill?
Oh, sad eyes; oh, sweet eyes,
why do you watch? Why do you kill?

There are hands, transparent palms,
color of snow like pale cotton hue;
there are sculptured arms
laced throughout with light blue.

Oh, sad eyes, sweet eye charms,
oh, lively crimson lips,
oh, white hands; oh lovely arms,
in thine grips,
I want to die in thine grips.

. . . 5-8-36

Rima (II)

Yo quiero ser el importuno sueño
que turba a media noche tu reposo;
yo quiero ser el céfiro nocturno
que juega con tu labio primoroso.

Pero duerme virgen angélica en silencio,
nada turbe tu sueño, blanca flor;
que voy a hacerme gota de tu sangre
¡para llegar hasta tu corazón!

. . . 5-5-36

Rhyme (II)[30]

I want to be the stubborn dream
that disturbs your midnight slumber;
I want to be the nighttime zephyr
that plays with your lovely lip seam.

But sleep silent angelic virgin tart,
nothing disturbs your sleep, white flower bud;
for I will become a drop of your blood
so I can reach up to your heart!

. . . 5-5-36

Rima (III)

Al cielo de tus ojos zarcos miro;
en tus pálidos manos yazco preso
y como Bécquer a su Julia digo
—¡Qué te diera por un beso!

Un mundo diera él por su mirada,
por su altiva sonrisa diera un cielo;
por sus labios, ¿quién sabe qué ofrendara
en el éxtasis loco de su anhelo?

Yo no tengo ni mundos (menos cielos)
y por eso
por un beso, mi vida, yo te ofrezco
otro beso.

. . . 6-30-36

Rhyme (III)[31]

Into the sky of your blue eyes I gaze;
in your pale hands I lay captive
and like Bécquer to his Julia I say—
Oh! For a kiss what I would give!

He would give a world for her,
for her proud smile he'd give a sky;
for her lips, who knows what he'd offer
in the crazy ecstasy of his desire?

I don't have worlds (nor skies either)
                    and because of this
for a kiss, my love, I can offer
                    just another kiss.

. . . 6-30-36

Song to Celia

Bríndame con tus ojos
y con los míos te brindaré.
O deja un beso dentro la copa;
más vino que ese no pediré.
La sed del alma para calmarse
divino pide que sea el licor;
mas si su néctar me diera Zeus,
tomara el tuyo como mejor.

Ha poco tiempo te mandé un ramo,
no sólo fué por hacerte honor
sino por ver si junto a tu lado
el ramo siempre quedara en flor.
Tú de las rosas sólo aspiraste
y el ramo luego volviste a mí.
Y desde entonces crece y —¡lo juro!
no huele a él mismo . . . ¡pues huele a ti!

. . . 3-31-36

(Pensamiento de Ben Jonson.)

Song to Celia[32]

Drink to me only with thine eyes,
And I will pledge with mine;
Or leave a kiss but in the cup,
And I'll not look for wine.
The thirst that from the soul doth rise
Doth ask a drink divine:
But might I of Jove's nectar sup,
I would not change for thine.
I sent thee, late, a rosy wreath,
Not so much honouring thee,
As giving it a hope that htere
It could not withered be.
But thou thereon didst only breathe
And sent'st it back to me,
Since when it grows, and smells, I swear,
Not of itself, but thee.

(By John Donne [1616].)

La tragedia del amor

The Tragedy of Love

Rima (IV)

Quién fuera rayo de blanca luna,
quién fuera lira de dulce voz,
quién fuera onda de la laguna
—¡quién fuera Dios!

Para bañarte con luz de plata,
acariciarte con mi agua azul,
para cantarte una serenata
—¡para saber si me quieres tú!

. . . 5-2-36

Rhyme (IV)[33]

Whoever would be ray of the white moon,
whoever would be the lyric of sweet sound,
whoever would be a ripple of the lagoon—
would be God!

To bath you with silver light shade,
to caress you with my water of blue,
to sing you a serenade—
just to know if you love me too!

. . . 5-2-36

A la suerte

¡Suerte! Suerte que sujetas
mi futuro a puño rudo,
¿por qué me hiciste poeta
si también me hiciste mudo?

Si de modo de expresar
lo que siento no soy dueño,
¿para qué me diste el alma?
¿para qué me diste el sueño?

¿Para qué impulso me diste
de mirar a las estrellas?
¿Para qué me hiciste triste
de desear las cosas bellas?

Si la estrella que yo veo
no la alcanzo —y más que el astro,
más lejano mi deseo
hacia cual siempre me arrastro.

¡Más lejano! ¡Qué desdicha
que en el mundo así me vea!
¡Como un Dante sin Beatrice!
¡Quijote sin Dulcinea!

¡Suerte, suerte, qué indiscreta
te has jugado tú conmigo!
Por haberme hecho poeta
¡te abomino! y te bendigo.

. . . mayo 1934

To Luck[34]

Luck! Luck who does subject
my future with fist of brute,
why did you make me a poet
if you also made me mute?

If the way I write and feel
does not belong to me,
Why did you give me soul?
Why did you let me dream?

Why did you make me glad
to gaze upon the starlings?
Why did you make me sad
for desiring beautiful things?

If the star I see above
is too far—and beyond a star's orbit,
more distant is my love
to which I'll always submit.

So distant! What curse
to be seen like this on earth!
Like a Dante with no Beatrice!
Quixote without Dulcinea's hearth!

Luck, luck how indiscrete
you have played a trick on me, too!
For having made me a poet
I hate you! And bless you, too.

. . . May 1934

Rima (V)

A pensar me pongo, a pensar
de todo lo que ha pasado,
del presente desgraciado,
del futuro que vendrá,

que amabas bien escuchar
ayer mis palabras necias
—reflejo que hoy me desprecias . . .
mañana —¿qué pasará?

. . . 11-7-35

Rhyme (V)[35]

I start to ponder, to ponder
about all that's come before,
about this present I abhor,
about the future yet to come,

that you really loved to hear
my stubborn expressions of yesterday—
I realize your rejection today . . .
tomorrow—what will come?

. . . 11-7-35

Musa

"Tras la hija ardiente de una visión".

¿A qué cantar el importuno ruego?
¿A qué ensanchar y restregar la herida?
¿Si sé que tienes corazón de acero
en tu cuerpo de diosa alabastrina?

Si sé que nunca te tendré en mis brazos,
si tú eres la fruta prohibida,
si existe entre ambos un inmenso lago,
¿por qué te canto en embriaguez divina?

Si tú ni me miras, ni me nombras,
¿por qué permito que mi amor se quede
en ti pensando por las tristes horas
cuando están a mi alcance otras mujeres?

¡No es a ti! ¡No eres tú lo que deseo,
altiva rapaza indiferente!
Es un sueño de amor lo que yo anhelo,
la fugaz ilusión que representas.

Hay otras que me ofrecen sus amores
y es el hombre, no el bardo, quien acepta.
Otras calmarán mis sedes de hombre
mas, ¡tú serás la amada del poeta!

. . . 4-25-36

Muse[36]

"In pursuit of the fiery daughter of a vision."

Why sing a useless appeal?
Why widen and rub the injury?
If I know you have a heart of steel
in your godly alabaster body?

If I know I'll never hold you close,
if you are the forbidden sweetness,
if a large lake lays between us,
why do I sing with divine drunkenness?

If you don't call or give that look of yours
why do I let my love to stay still
thinking of you for endless sad hours
when other women say they will?

It isn't you! You are not what I crave,
you child so proud and indifferent!
What I desire is a dream of love,
that fleeting illusion you represent.

There are others who offer their hearts
and its the man, not the bard, who will accept.
Others will satisfy my manly thirsts.
But, you will always be the love of this poet!

. . . 4-25-36

Rima (VI)

Recuerdos, recuerdos tristes,
recuerdos de media noche
—de mieles y de amarguras,
de alegrías y dolores.

Recerdos de ayer dichoso
que el pasado me arrebata,
recuerdos, dulces recuerdos
—¡ay, recuerdos que me matan!

. . . 5-4-36

Rhyme (VI)

Memories, sad memories,
memories of midnight—
of sweetness and bitterness,
of happiness and hurt.

Memories of happy yesterdays
that the past steals away,
memories, sweet memories—
Oh, those memories that slay!

. . . 5-4-36

Canta

A mi condiscípulo Roberto Ramírez R.

Entre fragantes y lucientes flores,
más bella que la pálida azucena,
yo te contemplo, angelical morena,
sultana del harén de mis amores.

Así le cantas tú a la bienquerida,
así le cantas tú, poeta-hermano,
y ella con su desdén y orgullo vano
deja en tu pecho herida sobre herida.

Mas ¿lloras? ¡canta! y si el dolor consume
tu pecho o te hiere como faca,
canta aún más ¿no sabes que la albahaca
le brinda al que la hiere su perfume?

Se ríe del dolor el alma fuerte
y ser alma poderosa es ser divino,
es ir por lo más alto del camino
que va desde la cuna hasta la muerte.

Pues canta, siempre canta, nunca llores,
así la fama te dará cien vidas
después de que se cierren tus heridas,
después de que se sequen ya sus flores.

. . . 8-25-35

Sing[37]

To my fellow classmate Roberto Ramírez R.

Between brilliant and fragrant flowers,
more beautiful than a white lilly's pale,
I adore you, beautiful brown angel,
sultanness from the harem of my lovers.

This is how you sing to the beloved,
this is how you sing, brother poet,
and she with her disdain and vain conceit
leaves your chest hurt and wounded.

But, why cry? Sing! And if pain consumes
your chest or wounds you like a sailor's spade,
sing even more, for don't you know a basil's blade
gives its perfume to the one who wounds?

A strong soul laughs at gloom
for to be a powerful soul is to be divine,
it is to travel the road's highest line
that goes straight from craddle to the tomb.

Well sing, always sing, never cry,
so fame will give you a hundred lives
long after your wound revives
long after your flowers finally go dry.

. . . 8-25-35

Carolina

Carolina, Carolina,
blanca estrella vespertina
que en el cielo resplandece
cuando el día ya declina.

Carolina, Carolina,
bella rosa de la China,
tu hermosura me embelece,
tu belleza me fascina.

Dicen que de amor carece
mi alma pútrida y cochina
mas de gozo se estremece
cuando digo . . . "Carolina".

. . . 2-15-35

Caroline[38]

Caroline, Caroline,
white star of nighttime
shining bright in the sky
as the day goes in decline.

Caroline, Caroline,
Chinese flower so divine,
your loveliness bewitches me,
your beauty excites the mind.

Love is absent some will say
from this rotten dirty soul of mine,
but it trembles full of joy
each time I whisper . . . "Caroline."

. . . 2-15-35

Ojos verdes

a Carolina

Ojos verdes, ojos verdes,
de suave mirar tan triste,
ojos que visten el alma
del color que el bosque viste.

Lagos verdes y profundos
con trazas de gris en ellos
do las nubes del cariño
reflejan sombra y destellos.

Ojos verdes, tristes, bellos
—tema de mi alabanza;
ojos color de follaje,
primavera y esperanza.

. . . *3-27-36*

Green Eyes[39]

For Caroline

Green eyes, green eyes,
of sad and soft stares,
eyes that dress the soul
the color a forest wears.

Green and deep lakes
and within them shades of gray
where clouds of love
reflect shadow and lightray.

Green eyes, sad, beauty—
object of my praise;
eyes the color of foliage,
hope and spring days.

. . . 3-27-36

Llueve

Llueve, llueve, gris el cielo,
gris como los ojos de ella;
hoy la noche no es la bella;
hoy la noche está de duelo.

Cabizbaja está la palma
bajo el golpe de agua y viento;
en el cuerpo frío siento
—pero más frío en el alma.

Y la luz en lontananza
más que'verse se adivina
tras la líquida cortina
—tal parece mi esperanza.

No hay del rayo voz ni huella;
sólo azota el agua fría;
llueve, llueve todavía
—así lloro yo por ella.

. . . 10-20-35

It Rains[40]

It rains, rains, the sky gray,
gray like those eyes of hers;
tonight the night is not ours;
tonight the night is mourning away.

The palm fronds fold
under blow of water and wind;
the cold I feel within—
but colder still inside my soul.

And the light far aways
one can only dream
behind the liquid seam—
this is how my hope sways.

No voice nor trace of light ray;
only cold water beating;
it rains, rains, unrelenting
for her this is how I cry.

. . . 10-20-35

Plumas negras

Un cuervo disfrazado de paloma
llegó hasta mi ventana un día,
cuando la luz, herida por la noche,
en los brazos de la tarde se moría . . .
y el rubio sol la obscuridad huía.

"Canta, paloma", yo le dije, "canta
—canta de su dicha y de la mía".
El ave abrió su pico a mi palabra
entonando tan negra letanía
que partióme el corazón cual hoja fría.

El cuervo ya voló de mi ventana
como voló de mi alma tu ternura
mas ha dejado aquí las plumas negras
—de azabache, como es la noche obscura. . .
negras, negras como es mi desventura.

. . . 10-29-35

Black Feathers

A crow disguised as a dove
came to my window one day,
when light, wounded by night,
lay dying in the noontime sway . . .
and from darkness the blond sun fled away.

"Sing dove," I said, "sing—
sing of your joy and mine."
The bird's beak awoke to my words
to sing such a dark rhyme
it broke my heart like a leaf in wintertime.

The crow has now flown my window
like your tenderness fled my soul's delight
but it has left its black feathers behind—
of darkest black, like the obscure night
black, black just like my plight.

. . . 10-29-35

Horas felices

"Ésas . . . ¡No volverán!"

Las horas felices ¡qué pronto pasaron!
cual las golondrinas de Bécquer se fueron.
Lanzáronse al aire; otras tierras buscaron
—dejando vacíos,
dejando vacíos los nidos de ayer.

¡Qué triste —qué solo el colegio sombrío!
¡qué extraños mis pasos que en él se pasearon!
parece una sala de juerga y de brillo
después de que todas las gentes marcharon.

Ya no volverán. ¡Qué palabras tan tristes!
tres gotas de hiel —tres Infiernos del Dante.
Y no volverás —¡tú mi amada que fuiste!
¡mi rubia sajona! ¡mi rosa fragante!

¡Adiós para siempre! Adiós, vida mía.
Son otras las tierras que pisan tus pies,
donde el español que tú amaras un día
muy poco se escucha entre el bárbaro inglés.

¡Colegio! Esfinge de tantos antaños
que has visto pasar en audaz desvarío
la ideal juventud, dime ¿has visto en tus años
amor como el nuestro? ¿Dolor como el mío?

¡Silencio! ¡Silencio! ¡Callad corazones!
Sé quieto mi pecho. ¡Cerrad cicatrices!
Ya siento en las quejas de viejas canciones
que todos lamentan sus horas felices.

Good Times[41]

"Those . . . will never return!"

Good times—how quickly they passed!
like Becquer's swallows they all fled.
Heaved into the sky; other lands they searched
leaving vacant
leaving vacant the nests of yesterday.

How sad—the school so lonely and somber!
how distant my steps that walked inside it!
It looks like a room for balls and laughter
after all the people have departed.

They will never return. Such sad prose!
Three drops of sorrow—three of Dante's Hells.
And you will never return—the one for whom I fell!
My Saxon blond! My fragrant rose!

Goodbye forever! My love, goodbye.
Upon other lands your feet walk
where the Spanish you will love one day
is hardly heard amid ugly English talk.

School! Sphynx of so many yesterdays
who has witnessed the audacious revelry
of ideal youth, tell me, have you seen in your days
a love like ours? Hurt like the one in me?

Silence! Silence! Quiet, you, my hearts!
Be still my chest. Heal, you, my scarlines!
I now know from old song parts
that everyone longs for their good times.

Las horas felices ¡qué pronto pasaron!
cual las golondrinas de Bécquer se fueron.
Lanzáronse al aire; otras tierras buscaron
—dejando vacíos,
dejando vacíos los nidos de ayer.

. . . 5-31-36

Good times—how quickly they passed!
like Becquer's swallows they all fled.
Heaved into the sky; other lands they searched
                    leaving vacant
leaving vacant the nests of yesterday.

. . . 5-31-36

May Queen

Una noche divina de mayo,
cual esa ninguna,
cuando ella era hermosa cual rayo
de pálida luna,

ella era reina de mayo,
su esclavo yo era,
el rudo, sumiso lacayo
y la bella altanera.

Ella era Reina del Baile
y yo era su payo
una noche divina de mayo . . .
de mayo, de mayo.

. . . 6-21-36

May Queen

A divine night in May,
unlike any other,
when she was beautiful as a ray
of pale moon glimmer.

She was the queen of May,
I was her slave,
the crude dutiful lackey
and she the beauty above.

She was Queen of the Dance
and I was her nave
a divine night in May . . .
in May, in May.

. . . 6-21-36

Azul y verde

Tornó aquel cielo azul que eran sus ojos
sobre el infierno verde de los míos;
todos mis sueños y mis desvaríos
vio sin espanto —todos mis abrojos.
Tornó aquel cielo azul que eran sus ojos
sobre el infierno verde de los míos.

Eran sus ojos cielo en primavera,
los míos verdes yunglas tropicales;
rodeado de mil sueños siderales,
mi espíritu enjaulado era una fiera.
Eran sus ojos cielo en primavera,
los míos verdes yunglas tropicales.

¡Qué claror en los cielos agrazones!
¡Cuanta fiera escondida en la maleza!
En sus ojos azules ¡qué pureza!
en los míos ¡qué sedes de pasiones!
¡Cuánta fiera escondida en la maleza!
¡Qué claror en los cielos agrazones!

. . . 6-27-36

Blue and Green[42]

She turned the blue sky of her eyes
upon the green inferno of mine;
all my dreams and raving mind
she saw without fear—all my frailties.
She turned the blue sky of her eyes
upon the green inferno of mine.

Her eyes were heaven in springtime sky,
my own a jungle of tropical greens;
surrounded by a thousand astral dreams,
my caged spirit was beastly
her eyes were heaven in springtime sky,
my own a jungle of tropical greens.

What clarity in these angry skies!
How many beasts hidden in the bush!
In her blue eyes—What a pure blush!
In mine—what passions arise!
So many beasts are hidden in the bush!
What splendor in these angry skies!

. . . 6-27-36

Rima (VII)

Si alguna vez en mi infeliz jornada
diera con ella
y grácil y sonriente la encontrara,
azul y bella.

La pena y el desvelo ocultaría
—el fuego vivo;
sin darle una mirada pasaría,
mudo y altivo.

Mas, si por mi senda de poeta,
mi extraña vida,
la llego a encontrar cual la saeta
rota y caída,

que los besos divinos de su boca
otros robaron,
que sus blondos cabellos otros hombres
acariciaron,

que no sé quién ha oído sus palabras
de ternura,
ni quién habrá llegado a estrecharla
de la cintura,

las hieles y las penas, las espinas
y los abrojos
en los cuales un día me arrastrara
por esos ojos;

todo, todo esto olvidaría
solo mirara

Rhyme (VII)[43]

If ever in my sad journey
    I came upon her
smiling and full of glee,
    blue with beautiful splendor.

My sorrow and longing I'd hide—
    the live flame;
without giving a glance I'd just ride
    voiceless and vain.

But, if in my path as a poet,
    my strange life,
I come to find her like a spent bullet
    fallen and rife,

that the divine kisses of her lips
    by others possessed,
that her blond hair in other men's grips
    carressed,

that I can't tell who has heard her voice
    of tenderness,
nor who has been able to squeeze
    her waist,

the sorrows and pains, the thorn
    and thistle ties
through which I once crawled tired and worn
    for those eyes;—

all, all of this I would forget
    just behold,

en que estaba caída, arrepentida
y abandonada.

No gastaría mis palabras
en vanos celos,
ni me exaltara vengativo
bajo los cielos.

Oiríamos los dos las melodías
de mis bulbules,
que al fin habían vuelto a mí sus tristes
ojos azules.

¡Ah! Si otra vez me la encontrara
por mi camino,
de todo, de todo me olvidara
por su cariño.

Si su alma viniera y me llamara
(y aún la espero)
todo el pasado se esfumara
en un "Te Quiero".

. . . 6-12-36

that she had fallen, full of regret
and abandoned old.

I would not waste my words
in vain jealousy,
nor would I gloat a vindictive sword
beneath blue sky canopy.

The two of us would hear the melodies
of my entreaty
that in the end her blue eyes
returned to me.

Oh! If I could find her once more
on my way,
all, all I would forget and more
for her love today.

If her soul would come and call
(and still I await her, too)
all the past would happily fall
with one—"I love you."

. . . 6-12-36

Vuelve la amada

Ojos míos, ojos míos,
digan, digan por piedad,
digan, digan que gozaron
otra vez de su beldad;
mis oídos, mis oídos,
(alabado sea Dios)
que hoy escuchan los acordes
musicales de su voz.
Que ha tornado, que ha tornado,
la que vi marcharse ayer,
y creí que nunca, nunca,
la vería más volver.

Labios míos, labios míos,
callen, callen por piedad;
no, no digan que me quiso,
labios cálidos, callad.
Ni un suspiro, ni un suspiro,
que mi amada ya olvidó
las palabras que le dije,
las miradas que me dió.
Sus caricias, cual los cantos
que en antaño le canté,
los arrebató el pasado
y el pasado ya se fué.

Lloren campos, lloren cielos,
llore todo como yo
que su cuerpo a mí ha venido
pero su alma —¡su alma no!

. . . 7-8-36

My Beloved Returns

Eyes of mine, eyes of mine,
tell me, for Gods' sake, tell me,
tell me, tell me you entwined
once more in her beauty;
ears of mine, ears of mine,
(praise be to the Lord)
for today you hear the chime
of her musical word.
She has arrived, she has arrived
the one I saw leave yesterday,
and that never, never could I believe
I'd see her back again today.

Lips of mine, lips of mine,
be quiet, for God's sake be quiet;
no, do not say she loved me fine,
warm lips, be silent.
Not a whisper, not a whisper
that my beloved forgot to see
the words I said to her,
the looks she gave to me.
Her caresses, like the song blasts
I sang to her yesterday,
were stolen by the past
and the past is no longer here.

Cry fields, cry sky,
everything cry like I do
that her body has returned to lay
but her soul—her soul has not come, too!

. . . 7-8-36

Primer amor

Cruzan otra vez por mi camino
los pies a los cuales me arrojé
—los labios que yo quise cuando niño,
los ojos en los cuales me miré.

¿Por qué te sonrojas? ¿Y tu triste
mirada dirijes hacia el pie?
¿Te da vergüenza decir que me quisiste?
¿O te hiere el pensar que yo te amé?

¡No recuerdes, por Dios, nuestros antaños!
La ilusión de esos tiempos ya se fue.
Ahora . . . soy un viejo de veinte años.
¿Tu edad? Nunca la supe y no la sé.

. . . 4-23-36

First Love

They pass again across my path
the feet to which I threw myself—
the lips that I loved throughout my youth
the eyes in which I saw myself.

Why do you blush? And sheppishly
turn your face to the floor?
Are you ashamed to say you loved me?
Or does it hurt to think I loved you more?

By God, don't you remember our yesterday!
The illusion of those times now dead.
Today . . . I am old at twenty.
Your age? I don't know and never did.

. . .4-23-36

L'amour

Si te hablan de amor, ¡ríete de ellos!
Es amor ilusión que se deshace;
el hombre es bestia burda, sus deseos
tu gracia frágil no los satisface.

¡Te miente! Y después abandonada
te deja con tu enjambre; vuelve cacho
a turbar la silencia madrugada
con risadas obscenas de borracho.

Sal para tu jardín, donde derrama
su pura luz el cielo de zafiro;
mira en la mustia rosa aquella araña
que labra solitaria su tejido.

. . . 1-18-36

(Pensamiento de Francis Jammes.)

L'amour[44]

If they speak of love, laugh at them!
Love is an illusion that fades away;
man is a crude beast, and his whim
your fragile grace can never satisfy.

He lies! And abandoned
he'll let you suffer alone; until his banter
disturbs the silent dawn
with drunk and dirty laughter.

Salt for your garden, where rains
the purple light of a sapphire sky
look at that spider as the rose wanes
that works its web solitarily.

. . . 1-18-36

(After Francis Jammes.)

Flor de burdel

¡Pobre mujer! Mujer de los burdeles,
vestida y coloreada cual el payo,
ocultas tu desdicha y tu desmayo
tras juergas, carcajadas y oropeles.

Jardín sin rosas, colmenar sin mieles,
lirio marchitado en pleno mayo,
no quiso Dios que antes partiera un rayo
al vil que te arrojó a los fangos crueles.

¡Flor de burdel! El ave pasajera
que añora el nido mas volver no alcanza,
alma extraviada y ya sin esperanza.

Ah, ¿cuál sería tu ilusión primera?
¿Dónde será tu tierra tan lejana?
¿De quién hija serás? ¿De quién hermana?

. . . 7-1-36

Bordello Flower[45]

Poor girl! Bordello girl,
dressed and painted like a clown,
you hide your pain and misfortune
behind parties, laughs and tinsel.

Garden without roses, hive without honey swirl,
a lilly in mid May that is withered down,
because God did not lift a hand
to beat the cruel beast who hauled you to hell.

Bordello flower! Bird with no rope
longing for a nest it can never reclaim,
lost soul and now without a hope.

Oh! What was your first dream?
Where could your distant land slope?
Whose daughter could you be? Sister to whom?

. . . 7-1-36

In memoriam

In Memory

Crossing the Bar

El crepúsculo . . . del véspero el fulgor . . .
¡y un claro llamar!
Que la barra no llore su dolor
cuando yo salga para el mar.

Que sea el flujo lento en su mover,
muy hondo para ruido y espumez,
cuando lo que del mar obtuvo ser
al mar vuelva otra vez.

El crepúsculo . . . y el toque de oración . . .
y después ¡la obscuridad!
Y que no se entristezca el corazón
cuando vaya yo a embarcar.

Porque aunque lejos, sobre el hondo mar,
sobre las aguas, yo navegaré,
con mi Piloto espérome enfrentar
cuando la barra ya cruzada esté.

. . . primavera 1933

(Pensamiento de Lord Tennyson.)

Crossing the Bar[46]

Sunset and evening star,
And one clear call for me!
And may there be no moaning of the bar,
When I put out to sea,

But such a tide as moving seems asleep,
Too full for sound and foam,
When that which drew from out the boundless deep
Turns again home.

Twilight and evening bell,
And after that the dark!
And may there be no sadness of farewell,
When I embark;

For tho' from out our bourne of Time and Place
The flood may bear me far,
I hope to see my Pilot face to face
When I have crossed the bar.

. . . Spring 1933

(By Lord Tennyson.)

Soneto escrito el 25 de mayo

Cual fruta que por modo artificial
en poco tiempo adquiere madurez,
tu mente nunca supo la niñez,
aun joven fuiste serio y judicial.

Cual flor de nacimiento tropical
que pronto se abre y con igual presteza
marchita y triste inclina la cabeza
al polvo que hace todo —todo igual.

Igual que flor o fruta tu vivir
muy pronto'terminó en la muerte fría.
No temas que al dejar de existir

mi voz no más entona tu elegía
—Los cielos, al saber de tu partir,
¡lloraron en torrentes este día!

. . . 5-25-33

Sonnet Written on the 25th of May[47]

Like a fruit through means artificial
is rushed to reach its ripeness,
your mind never wore a child's dress,
though young you were serious and judicial.

Like a flower born in places tropical
that quickly blooms and with the same promptness
withers and bows its head in sadness
towards the dust that makes all—all equal.

Same as fruit or flower your living
quickly concluded in cold death.
Do not fear that after you cease being

your elegy will stop giving my voice breathe—
the heavens that learned of your leaving,
cried that day a torrential wreath!

. . . 5-25-33

Epitafio

Gastóse muy pronto la vela encendida,
Allá por el aire la esencia veloz
Botando la tierra subió dolorida
Robando a nosotros su faz y su voz.
Instante tan corto que encierra una vida;
Es hilo de seda que al alma guardó.
La muerte le entabla la lucha reñida . . .

Mas, débil el hilo, la muerte triunfó.

. . . junio 1933

Epitaph[48]

Gone too quickly the burning flame,
Away through the air his speeding essence
Bouncing the earth it arose in pain
Robbing us of his face and his voice.
Instant so short where life is contained;
Enclosed in silk thread the soul is held.
Life's ferocious fight by death detained. . .

More, the thread was so weak, death prevailed.

. . . June 1933

Rosa

¡Rosa que en la tumba naces
de mi desdichada hermana!
Dime, flor de brava grana
—dime, ¿cuándo te deshaces?

Rosa . . . de su cuerpo brotas;
eres ser de sus despojos.
Quizá de sus bellos ojos
nacen tus hojitas rotas.

Mas, aunque cortarte quiero
yo te dejo; que a la hermosa
pronto la recoge, rosa,
el Eterno Jardinero.

. . . verano 1933

Rose[49]

Rose that in the grave is born
of my unfortunate sister!
Tell me, brave seeded flower—
tell me, when will you be undone?

Rose . . . from her body you flow;
a being made of her remains.
Perhaps it is from her lovely eyes
that your torn leaves grow.

But, though I want to prune
I let you be; for the beautiful beloved,
rose, will soon be harvested,
by the Eternal Gardener soon.

. . . Summer 1933

A Blanca

"En tierra lejana tengo yo una hermana. . ."

Quisiera que mi genio de poeta
fuera más vasto que el azul lejano;
así pudiera mi inspirada mano
decir lo que se mueve en mi alma inquieta.

Mi voz volara entonces cual saeta
en busca de tu sombra en el arcano.
Pero mi sueño de cantarte es vano
porque el dolor del cuello me sujeta.

Cual golpe de puñal, mortal y rudo,
hiere mi pecho tal angustia fría
que me congela y que me deja mudo.

Y una lágrima, clara como el día,
resbálase al papel blanco y desnudo . . .
mi único tributo y poesía.

. . . marzo 1934

To Blanca[50]

"In distant lands I have a sister . . ."

I wish that my poetic talent
were greater than the distant blue sky;
this way my inspired hand could say
what moves inside my restless spirit.

My voice would fly like an arrow sent
to search for your shadow in the past gone by.
But my dream of singing to you is obsurdity
because the pain in my brain does not relent.

Like a dagger's stab, mortal and brute,
it wounds my chest with such cold agony
that freezes my hand and leaves me mute.

And a tear, clear as the day sky,
slides down to the paper white and nude . . .
my only tribute and poetry.

. . . March 1934

La voz rebelde

The Rebellious Voice

Rima (VIII)

Id y venid, las ondas de los mares;
romped sobre las playas en espuma.
Toda la dicha del vivir se esfuma;
sed lentos y sed tristes mis cantares.
Id y venid, las ondas de los mares;
romped sobre las playas en espuma.

. . . 6-26-36

Rhyme (VIII)[51]

Do come and go, you ocean waves;
break, you, over the beaches in foam.
All the joy of living vanishes;
do be slow and sad, too, my songs.
Do come and go, you ocean waves;
break, you, over the beaches in foam.

. . . 6-26-36

Lágrimas de ceniza

Noche domina al cielo;
sobre sus campos pisa . . .
lágrimas sin consuelo,
lágrimas de ceniza . . .

Golpe que se ha curado
deja sus cicatrices;
flama que se ha apagado
deja cenizas grises.

¿Símbolos del quebranto?
¿del arrepentimiento?
¿signos de amargo llanto?
Eso no es lo que siento.

Hay lágrimas de fuego
que de pasión se exprimen;
hay lágrimas que luego
de ese calor se eximen,

lágrimas apacibles,
mudas, silencias, frías,
de penas indecibles,
lágrimas cual las mías.

. . . agosto 1933

Tears of Ash

Night dominates heaven;
over dark fields it marches . . .
tears without consolation,
tears of ashes.

Blow that has healed
leaves scar lashes;
flame that has extinguished
leaves grey ashes.

Symbols of suffering?
Or repentance?
Signs of bitter weeping?
That is not what I sense.

There are tears of fire
that from passion are squeezed;
there are tears that later
from that heat are released,

gentle tears,
mute, silent, frozen,
of untold sorrows,
tears like mine.

. . . August 1933

Letanía

Lento, lento va mi canto,
nada, nada de alegría;
este mes y en este día
fué la fecha en que nací.

Lenta, lenta va mi vida,
tanta lágrima y gemido
—que si no hubiera nacido
no tuviera que sufrir.

. . . 9-3-34

Litany[52]

Slow, slow goes my song,
nothing, nothing of joy;
this month and on this day
was the date I was ushered.

Slow, slow goes my life,
so many tears and a moan—
that if I had never been born
I would not have suffered.

. . . 9-3-34

Rima (IX)

Duran nuestras vidas una hora
y nuestro ser,
cual nota de la cítara arrancada,
muere al nacer.

Se pierde en el fondo de la nada
cual voz fugaz.
El hombre es una bestia soñadora
y nada más.

. . . 4-26-36

Rhyme (IX)[53]

One hour our lives last
and our being,
like a note from the *cítara* torn,
dies while birthing.

It is lost at the bottom of oblivion
like a fleeting voice.
Man is a daydreaming beast
and nothing else.

. . . 4-26-36

Rima (X)

¡Ay, las pasiones que moran
y se esconden en la calma!
cuando los ojos no lloran
y se sangra y llora el alma.
¡Ay, las pasiones que moran
y se esconden en la calma!

¡Ay, de los labios callados!
pero ¿quién calla al recuerdo?
por no morderme los labios,
pobre corazón, te muerdo.
¡ay, de los labios callados!
pero ¿quién calla al recuerdo?

. . . 7-15-35

Rhyme (X)[54]

Oh, the passions that reside
and hide beneath the surface!
When eyes hide tears inside
and the soul bleeds and cries.
Oh, the passions that reside
and hide beneath the surface!

Oh, of those silent lips!
But who keeps memory quiet?
To not bite my lips,
poor heart, it is you I bite.
Oh, of those silent lips!
But who keeps memory quiet?

. . . 7-15-35

Rima (XI)

¡Ah, Dios! ¡Ah, Dios! ¡Qué abismo tan profundo!
Más convencido estoy de que no existes;
¿Cómo puedes permitir en este mundo
cosas tan injustas y tan tristes?

. . . 7-28-36

Rhyme (XI)

Oh God! Oh God! What abyss so profound!
I'm more convinced you don't exist;
how can you allow on the ground
things so sad and unjust?

. . . 7-28-36

Nocturno

De noche, cuando pongo la cabeza
sobre la almohada, mas dormir no puedo,
cuando cae el rocío en su pureza
y el viento va quejándose muy quedo,

cual sombras de loco desvarío,
cual mirajes en áridos desiertos,
veo brillar en torno mío
los pálidos rostros de los muertos.

Sí, veo las faces luminosas
de aquellos que ya son podredumbre
y me brindan miradas cariñosas,
sus ojos anima extraña lumbre.

¿Serán las leves manos de la brisa?
¿la gran tristeza innata de mi alma?
mas yo también les doy una sonrisa
al verles sonreír con tanta calma.

Y siempre entre todas se ha lucido
de mi hermana menor la faz morena;
ha varias noches ya que ha aparecido
otra faz nueva, plácida y serena.

¡Malditos los dioses imponentes!
¡la Mano que al vil del golpe esquiva!
¡malhayan mis brazos impotentes!
permiten aún que un monstruo viva.

Y llora mi espíritu sombrío,
florecen en mi alma los desiertos,
cuando veo brillar en torno mío
los pálidos rostros de los muertos.

. . . 6-18-36

Nocturne[55]

By night, when my head lay
on the pillow, but cannot sleep,
when dew drops innocently
and the wind complains with a weep,

like shadows of crazy insanity,
like mirages in dry wasteland,
I see shine all around me
the pale faces of the dead.

Yes, I see the luminous faces
of those now rotted lame
and they offer tender glances,
their eyes animate a strange flame.

Are they the light hands of a breeze?
The great innate sadness of my soul?
For I, too, smile to please
at seeing the ease of their own smile

And always among them all has glowed
my younger sister's brown face;
for many nights now it has showed
a new, placid and serene grace.

Damned those imposing Gods!
The Hand that dodges the striking evil!
Useless my impotent hands!
They still allow a beast to live.

And my somber spirit will cry,
as deserts in my soul bud,
while I see shine all around me
the pale faces of the dead.

. . . 6-18-36

Rima (XII)

¡Quisiera llorar pero no puedo!
Las lágrimas no acuden a mis ojos . . .
¡Dios Impasible! ¿Eres destino ciego
o niño cruel que juegas con nosotros?

A media noche, cuando solo estaba
en el silencio muerto de mi alcoba
una noche de abril de luna clara,
cuando reina el Sueño entre las frías horas,
cuando lloran las almas destrozadas,
y el mismo viento —que no siente— llora,
viendo en cruento desfile mi quebranto,
¡Llora! —le dije al corazón herido.
Y el corazón me contestó así sollozando—
Ya no puedo llorar . . . ¡ahora maldigo!

. . . 4-20-36

Rhyme (XII)[56]

I'd like to cry but I can't!
Tears don't well in my eyes . . .
Uncaring God! Are you blind fate
or a cruel child who plays with us?

At midnight, while all alone
in the dead silence of my room
one April night with a clear moon,
when sleep reins amid the cold gloom,
when all the shattered souls are crying,
and the very wind—that cannot feel—cries, too,
at seeing my bloody sorrow parading,
Cry!—I told my wounded heart to do.
And he answered back sobbing—
I can no longer cry . . . Curse is all I do!

. . . 4-20-36

Décimas[57]

Décimas

A don Gonzalo Casas Gutiérrez

Gracias a Ud., don Gonzalo,
amigo desconocido,
mil perdones yo le pido
por mi verso trunco y malo.

1.

Décimas nunca escribí:
he usado el heroico verso,
el soneto corto y terso,
romances aquí y a allí;
y nunca, nunca creí
que yo llegaría a usarlo
mas sus versos recibí
y mi entendimiento ralo
espoleo al dar aquí
gracias a Ud., don Gonzalo.

2.

La fama es una mujer
de esas de vida galante,
el triunfo es un vil bergante
de nefando proceder;
qué lejos está el ayer,
Las estrellas —¡ay, qué lejos!
desde este mundo dormido
do las miramos perplejos
las miramos perplejos
amigo desconocido.

Décimas[58]

For Don Gonzalo Casas Gutiérrez

Many thanks, Don Gonzalo, sir,
my unknown friend of rhymes,
I ask your pardon a thousand times
for my bent and very bad verse.

1.

These décimas I never wrote:
I have used the heroic word,
the sonnet terse and short,
here and there a romance I wrote;
and never, never had I thought
that I could write it any worse
then your verse I read alot
and my weak skills at writing verse
I now spur and struggle to plot
Don Gonzalo, many thanks, sir.

2.

Fame is a woman truly grand
like those of high society,
triumph a vile scoundrel for he
is very poorly born and bred;
yesterday is so far away,
The stars—Oh, how far removed!
from this sleeping world today
where we look at them amazed
we look at them with amazed
my unknown friend of rhymes.

3.

Es verdad que yo anoté
lo que triunfo le han llamado,
que de bronce bien tallado
la medalla mía fué;
mas la verdad le diré:
rey tuerto entre ciegos fuí
pues en la tierra de aquí
se echa la Lengua al olvido . . .
dejaré de hablar así,
mil perdones, yo le pido.

4.

Ya mundano o sideral,
siempre busco ir sereno,
corriendo tras de lo bueno
y topando con el mal;
espero en mi capital
contar ya con otro amigo
y por mi camino sigo
tratando de hacer un halo
(tratando de hacerlo digo)
con mi verso trunco y malo.

. . . 7-11-36

3.

It is true that I have attained
what some have called fortune,
cast in fine bronze with fashion
the medal is mine I proclaimed
but the real truth I must exclaim:
one-eyed king amid the blind I sat
because on this earth I must note
the Tongue is thrown without designs . . .
But I'll stop talking of this rut,
I ask your pardons a thousand times.

4.

Whether mundane or celestial,
I always seek to be serene.
running after things pristine
and bumping into evil;
I hope that in my capital
to come across another friend
and on my journey I will wind
trying to make a starburst
(trying to make it so I said)
with my bent and very bad verse.

. . . 7-11-36

L'envoi[59]

Al cumplir veintiún años

Detente, Tiempo, en tu veloz carrera;
mira hacia atrás a mi niñez perdida;
detén aún la mano que convida
hacia el futuro ignoto que me espera.

¡Quién fuera mago! ¡quién un sabio fuera
para leer el libro de la Vida,
para encontrar la clave allí escondida
que todo el Gran Secreto me dijera! . . .

Mi alma, si por tu camino triste
se derrumban tus sueños y tus dioses,
olvídalos. Recuerda que eres fuerte.

Calza de seda pero hierro viste;
y sigue así hasta que tu planta poses
en los portales fríos de la Muerte.

. . . 9-3-36

Upon Turning Twenty-One[60]

Stop, Time, your fast race;
turn back to my lost infancy;
stop, too, the hand that invites me
towards the unknown future maze.

Oh, that I were a magician! Someone wise
so the book of Life would open to me,
so I could find the hidden key
and the Grand Plan I could recognize! . . .

My soul, if on your sad trail
your dreams and gods collapse,
forget them. Remember your strength.

Wear silk for shoes but dress in steel
and continue until your sole steps
through the cold portals of Death.

. . . 9-3-36

Addenda

El Pocho[61]
(1836-1936)

En tu propio terruño serás extranjero
por la ley del fusil y la ley del acero;

y verás a tu padre morir balaceado
por haber defendido el sudor derramado;

verás a tu hermano colgado de un leño
por el crimen mortal de haber sido trigueño.

Y si vives —acaso— será sin orgullo,
con recuerdos amargos de todo lo tuyo;

tus campos, tus cielos, tus aves, tus flores
serán el deleite de los invasores;

para ellos su fruto dará la simiente,
donde fueras el amo serás el sirviente.

y en tu propio terruño serás extranjero
por la ley del fusil y la ley del acero.

(1936)

Alma pocha[62]

Alma pocha
ensangrentada,
la sufrida,
la olvidada,
la rebelde sin espada;
alma pocha
salpicada
de tragedia y humorada,
alma pocha.

En tu propio terruño serás extranjero
por la ley del fusil y la ley del acero;
y verás a tu padre morir balaceado
por haber defendido el sudor derramado;
verás a tu hermano colgado de un leño
por el crimen mortal de haber sido trigueño.
Y si vives —acaso— será sin orgullo,
con recuerdos amargos de todo lo tuyo;
tus campos, tus cielos, tus aves, tus flores
serán el deleite de los invasores;
para ellos su fruto dará la simiente,
donde fueras el amo serás el sirviente.
y en tu propio terruño serás extranjero
por la ley del fusil y la ley del acero.

De este modo
habló el destino
en la jornada tejana
¡y la boca se envilece
con el nombre de Santa Anna!
Alma pocha
vas llorando
la vergüenza mexicana.

Alma pocha,
alma noble y duradera,
la que sufre,
la que espera.

(1936)

Annotations

[1] As noted in the introduction, we have chosen to translate "adolescencia" as "youth" due to the collection's overall existentialist concerns, instead of "adolescent," which has the more sociological and medical resonance Paredes invokes in the second paragraph of his Prologue. In our translation of the Prologue, however, we used "adolescent" and "youth" based on the specific context of its usage. In some cases, he describes "adolescencia" in terms of a physical phenomenon, that is, a stage in one's biological and social life. In others, the term is best translated by the more general temporal and connotative "youth," which allows for the metaphysical and existentialist themes that run throughout the text.

In the second paragraph, we chose to translate "niño," which in Spanish refers to children of either gender, as "boy" because of the autobiographical nature of the Prologue and subsequent verse.

There is no date for the Prologue noted in the original manuscript, however, we assume that it must have been written after the latest dated poem, "*Al cumplir veintiún años* / Upon Turning Twenty-One," which is the final composition of the collection that bears the date September 3, 1936. All extant bibliographical materials date the publication of the manuscript as 1937, several months after the last poem.

[2] A possible translation of this subheading would be "Patriortic Lyric." However, we chose "Lyre" for several reasons. First, it alludes to the musicality that informs much of the verse in the manuscript overall. Moreover, stringed instruments based on the lyre such as the guitar and violin figure prominently in Paredes' verse. The use of "Lyre" also seems particularly appropriate given the neoclassical (and perhaps nascent Orientalist) semiotics of the cover, which features an oil lamp exuding a trail of smoke that travels up towards a satyr playing a flute.

Lyre gains added resonance from the pun created by "lyre" and "liar." A significant aspect of Paredes' project as an intellectual and artist was the retelling of history from a variety of perspectives, which inevitably raises "truth" as a trope. Finally, it is important to note that in some colloquial contexts, "lira" also means *guitarra*, or guitar, which was one of Paredes' favored instruments and the instrument used to play Mexican folk ballads like *corridos*.

[3] Paredes' attempt to create a consonant rhyme scheme of alternating lines in the original Spanish poem is not preserved in lines 3 and 15. In our translation, we took the liberty of rhyming alternating stanzas. Our use of contractions in lines 5 and 7 are more informal than the original but their use enables us to facilitate ryhythm. This preference for rhythm is important given that this entire section is inaugurated by an allusion to music ("lira").

On line 4, we chose to translate the Spanish term "patria" as homeland" instead of "country" because the former connotes more intimacy between the poetic persona and Mexico, which is the land being claimed. As noted in the introduction, we have chosen to use "country" in some poems when the connotation of the poem involved a simple description of Mexico as a political entity separate from the poetic persona's claim to it. See the introduction for further discussion of this trope.

On like 14, we used "foreign" (*estranjera*) instead of "strange" for Paredes' term *extraña* because "foreign" has the geopolitical resonance that Paredes is invoking while also preserving the sense of "strangeness" and alienation.

[4] The assonant rhyme scheme of this poem is not preserved in lines 9 and 11 (ababab / cbdbeb), although line 11 does have a consonant rhyme with its corresponding line 7 that opens the second stanza. Our translation recuperates Paredes' apparent intention of rhyming alternating lines while also attempting to replicate the rhythm of the overall poem, which connotes song. For a discussion of the song trope, see the introduction.

The term *montes* on line 7 literally means "hills," but the context appears to suggest the somewhat false cognate, "mountains." Also, we translate the line as "crowned with alabaster" even though Paredes' characterization uses an irregular article *de* instead of *con* (with), which would be more syntactically sound in Spanish. We made slight syntax changes in line 10 to preserve the new rhyme scheme. We translate *poesía* in Paredes' original footnote as "poem" since the reference is to the specific poem even though *poesía* also has a broader plural resonance in Spanish.

[5] The original Spanish title of this poem presents several translation options. The Spanish term *illusión* is somewhat of a false cognate for "illusion," which has a slightly negative connotation in English. The poem's tone actually vacillates between a somber expression of longing (such as an "illusion") and a celebratory affirmation of the poetic persona's Mexicanness (more of a "dream" or "vision"). We have chosen to use the word "illusion" in order to preserve the ambiguity that, in the context of the overall corpus, is distinguished by the teleology of exile literature. Indeed, even though

Paredes was born and raised on the U.S. side of the U.S.-Mexico border, his themes still resonate with the ethos of the school of Mexican literature and culture known as *México de afuera*, or "Mexico from afar." That is, the poet's claims to affiliation always already are surrounded by the aura of nostalgia that belies the realities of Chicana/o deterritorialization. In immigrant and exile literature, of which this text is related, longing is accompanied by realizations that this longing also implies loss and an elusive, if not illusionary, or perhaps even delusional, hope of reclamation.

We have attempted to replicate the rhyme scheme of the original Spanish poem, which involves rhymes between the first and fourth, and also the second and third lines of eacg stanza (abba /cddc, etc.). This required strategic syntax and word choice changes.

Other translation challenges arise from Paredes' unorthodox spelling. For instance, on line 4, *ha tiempo*, should be spelled *a tiempo*. If the line is meant to suggest exasperation or a lament, such as "all this time" or "such time," "what a time," or even "so much time," then it normally would have been spelled as *¡qué tiempo!* or *¡tánto tiempo!* On the other hand, the *ha* might suggest the simple passage of time, as in *que ha pasado tiempo*, or "so much time has passed." We used the former option. Paredes uses this ambiguous term in other poems, which we similarly translated in context.

The Spanish term *raza* also is a false cognate of "race." The term denotes "people" while still connoting a culturally, ethnically, and perhaps even biologically distinct "race." Nonetheless, we have chosen to use "race" in order not to lose the allusions to race and racial conflicts that permeate throughout Paredes' poetic, literary, and scholarly corpus. The *nopal*, or prickly pear cactus, is a specific type of cactus. We have chosen to use the Spanish term because it is common knowledge in South Texas. The alternatives—prickly pear or cactus—further detract from the rhythm of the poem.

On line 6, in order to preserve the rhyme, we have replaced the original *sajon* with "English" instead of the more literal "Saxon." *Sajón* is commonly used by Paredes to refer to Anglo Americans and Euroamericans in general in this collection, whereas in the poems included in *Between Two Worlds*, he uses the epithet *gringa*. On line 13, we translate *querellas* as "in disdain" because the context suggests more of a complaint than "desires" or "wants," which are the literal meanings of the original Spanish term. On line 28, we chose to use neuter pronouns in the English translation except when the gendered Spanish pronouns refer to a specific person.

Dr. Nemesio García Naranjo was a former member of Mexican President Victoriano Huerta's cabinet during the Mexican Revolution. He was originally from Monterrey, Nuevo León, and was known as a political reactionary. After the fall of Huerta's regime, García Naranjo went into exile and settled in San Antonio, Texas, where he became a patron of Mexican culture and the arts, especially of young Mexican and Mexican-American poets. Neither the text of the presentation alluded to above, nor any correspondence between Paredes and Dr. García Naranjo, has been found in the Américo Paredes Papers. The García Naranjo Papers are archived with Arte Público Press at the University of Houston.

[6] The rhyme scheme in the original Spanish is highly irregular (abbba / cdcaccaadef, etc.). Nonetheless, there is an internal rhythm to the poem that we tried to preserve in our translation, which roughly revolves around a consonant rhyme scheme of alternating lines.

The Spanish *vago* on line 9 could be an abbreviation of *vagabondo*, which suggests a "vagrant." However, we chose the term "wandering" because the English cognate, "vagrant" has too many negative connotations that do not apply to the heroic subject of the poem, which ultimately is a paean to General Simon Bolivar, the 19th-century Venezuelan who envisioned a unified Latin American nation.

We also took other liberties with tense and plurals to accentuate the rhythm and epic heroic tone of the poem.

[7] *La Chinaca* alludes to a style of dress known as *La China Poblana*, which roughly translates as the "Puebla Chinese Style." According to Ramón Saldívar (2006), this style apparently arose in the 19th century as a peudo-indigenous cultural challenge to the sympathizers of French occupation of Mexico. We decided to preserve the title in Spanish because it is a commonly understood folk form, style and song. The Paredes Papers contain a playbill that also indicate this to be the moniker of a famous Mexican singer who may have inspired the poem (see Figure 18).

Since the consonant rhyme scheme of the original Spanish is not preserved throughout the poem, we sought to mimic the rhythm of the poem instead of attempting to replicate the alternating stanza rhymes.

On line 5, we chose to use the Spanish term *ranchera*, for reasons explained in the introduction. This popular Mexican musical form is distinguished by its mariachi string and horn accompaniment. Its lyrics usually span a broad range of topics, but they always maintain a regular scheme: verse-chorus-verse-chorus-verse.

The *zenzontli* referenced on line 40 is the indigenous name for a Mexican blackbird that belongs to the Passeriformes genus. This bird has brownish or grayish plumage and a white belly and is renowned for imitating the songs on other birds.

The term *remexicana*, which appears throughout the poem, is translated as a superlative. That is, instead of referring to a specific song or genre, it appears to be a neologism that implies "that very Mexican song, " or rather, "the epitome of Mexican songs."

There is an inexplicable space between stanzas 7 and 8 that we attribute to typographical errors. In our version we separate these stanzas.

8 *Corridos* are octosyllabic acoustic ballads that can be divided into a variety of genres. They usually involve an invocation, in which the singer, traditionally a male, asks permission to recount a tale. This is followed by an exposition, conflict resolution, and a *despedida*, or farewell, in which the singer closes the song with a didactic commentary on the events recounted by the performance. It is not a danceable form, but rather, usually serves as a form of oral history. As noted in the introduction, Paredes is renowned for his recovering of *El corrido de Gregorio Cortez* ("The Ballad of Gregorio Cortez"), which is an epic heroic corrido.

Huapangos are a type of tropical *son* (see below) developed mainly within the coastal state of Veracruz, Mexico, though it also is common in other Mexican states. A traditional *huapango* usually requires a violin, a *jarana* (small 8-string solo guitar) and a *huapanguera* (large guitar). Its topics are as diverse as the son and the "New *Huapango*" genre mixes *son huasteco* with *ranchera* music.

Yucatecas are characteristic of the Yucatan Peninsula in southern Mexico. They regularly keep a simple rhythm and are almost always played by a trio.

The *son* is a popular music genre developed in Mexico during the Colonial period and also various analogues throughout the Caribbean. It includes several main features such as the *zapatadeado* (heal stomping rhythm) along with a combination of instrumental music and singing. Similar to the *corrido*, the *son* is made up of couplets containing verses of eight syllables.

9 The *paso doble* (roughly translated as "two step" though it bears little resemblance to the U.S. country music dance form of the same name) is a vivacious march of Spanish origin that is highly popular in Mexico and Latin America. The form is in duple meter and one of its characteristics is its change in colorful modulation. Due to the movements required, the *paso doble* is considered a fine ballroom dance like the waltz. This poem, which Paredes composed as a variation of the Petrachan Sonnet, has a particularly ironic resonance given its simultaneous rejection and performance of European colonial legacy in the Americas. Paredes is somewhat loose with his invocation of the form; the traditional Petrarchan sonnet is written as abba / abba / cdc / cdc, while Paredes' version is written as: abba / abba // ccd / eed. The pattern of our translation is abba / abba / eef / ggh.

10 The *Rumba*, which also can be spelled *Rhumba*, is a popular Cuban and Caribbean dance with African roots. *Madrigals* (roughly translated as "morning songs") are short rhyming poetic compositions of seven or eleven syllables. They usually have an amorous theme and are adapted for

musical performances with several voices. A typical *madrigal* is made with two or three stanzas of three verses and two verses with a different rhythm. *Aguardiente* is an alcoholic beverage made from sugar cane. It is a poor quality drink that also is bitter like whiskey.

As with many of Paredes' sonnets, this Petrarchan sonnet varies in the final sestet (abba / abba / cdc / dcd). Our translation of this poem corresponds to Paredes' rhyme scheme.

[11] This Petarchan sonnet begins with the same first line of a similarly-themed poem published in English under the title "Night," by the (Harlingen) *Valley Morning Star* on May 3, 1934. A facsimile of this publication is included as Figure 9. These two poems correspond to several of Paredes' "Night" poems, one of which is included in this section.

[12] This English version of *El Rio Bravo* is Paredes' original 1934 composition. According to his footnote in *Between Two Worlds*, this poem originally was published in the (Harlingen) *Valley Morning Star* in October 1934, before being reprinted in *BTW* in 1991. The *Valley Morning Star* printed several other poems by Paredes, which the poet notes was ironic given that the editors of the paper also were extremely racist at the time. As indicated, the Spanish version of the poem published in *Cantos de adolescencia* is dated two years later, July 12, 1936. See introduction for further discussion of this poem.

[13] This poem appears to have been begun as a sonnet, but ultimately has an irregular rhyme scheme that is recurrent throughout the collection (abba / cddc / effe). We made some tense and syntax changes to approximate the rhythm of the original.

[14] This poem has an irregular rhyme scheme in the original (ababced / ceed). Instead of attempting to replicate it, we chose to create a translation that contained its own internal rhythm, which resulted in a slightly different scheme (abbabcd / ceec).

[15] As with other Petrarchan Sonnets by Paredes, we made several tense and syntax changes to preserve the form. We chose not to translate *tarde* as the literal "afternoon" because other allusions in the poem suggest the time just before nightfall instead of noontime. While "Autumn's Afternoon" has an alliterative sound, "Autum's Evening" is more appropriate because of the somber intimations in the poem. Paredes set this poem to music, and a facsimile of his original score is included as Figure 47. Evidence indicates that Paredes also composed this poem in English, but the version apparently is lost.

[16] This is another poem that appears to be modeled on a Petarchan Sonnet. However, Paredes adds an extra line to what would serve as the second quartet. In order to retain the rhythmic pattern we made tense and word choice changes. This included some wide variations, such as adding the

adjective "holy" in line 6, extending "meadow holly" for *prado* in line 7, and extrapolating "guitar rattles its hollows" in line 13, for *La guitarra se desata*, which roughly translates as the guitar "loosens" or "unleashes." All these changes remain true to the content and context.

17 This poem, an existentialist meditation that recurs throughout the collection, resonates with the despair of Paredes' contemporary, César Vallejo, whose inaugural collection *Heraldos Negros* ("Black Heralds"), which the poet would have known. This poem shares its title with a published English poem that is included as Figure 9. See also *Nocturno* ("Nocturne") in Part VII of the collection.

18 We took various liberties with syntax and in the use of English colloquialisms in translating this canto. We also translated the original rhyme scheme (abbc / abbc) to abab / abab) to give the translation its own internal rhythm.

19 As noted in the introduction, we attempted to parallel Paredes' vernacular idiom. "Pantaloon" is a stock character in Italian Renaissance drama, specifically *La comedia del arte* genre, which is characterized by its comedic look at love. Pantaloon also appears in Shakespeare's play, *The Twelfth Night*. In this play, he generally is a dim-witted ruffian who feigns sophistication but only succeeds at illustrating his crudeness, arrogance and ignorance. Pantaloon is, in effect, a comedic version of the picaresque antihero.

In this poem, we changed the original rhyme scheme (from abba / cddc / aeea to abba / bccb / affa). We also took other liberties with the colloquial spellings in an attempt to approximate Paredes' use of vernacular diction.

20 We chose to translate the referent as "girl" because of the juvenile context of the overall collection. The vernacular English term actually would be "white girl," but "Anglo" would be the closest translation for the 1930s South Texas context of the poem's composition. If the referent had been identified more definitively as *una mujer*, we would have translated the title as "For An Anglo Woman." We changed the last stanza of the sestet of the original Petrarchan sonnet (from cdc / dcd to cdc / cdc) to preserve the rhyme.

21 In this poem, we attempted to approximate the diction and tone of the Renaissance neoclassicism that undergirds the theme and style of Paredes' original composition. This poem, in fact, appears to arise from Paredes' study of the Greek classics as an undergraduate and graduate student. This neoclassical fable, which is undergirded by a carpe diem telos, also illuminates the neoclassical allusion of the original cover.

22 In this translation we do not present a parallel rhyme scheme because it is so irregular (abab / cdcdc / dbeaae / baab) that it appears Paredes was only

attemping to rhyme idiosyncratically as opportunity allowed. We did, however, attempt to preserve some links between stanzas, which creates foregrounding effect of the original. We also took some liberties with syntax to create an internal rhythm.

[23] This is one of two poems titled *Jugete*/Toy. To avoid confusion, we have numbered them. This poem has a more systematic rhyme sceme (abba / acca / bddb / beeb / affa), which we attempted to preserve in our translation. This required that we take some liberties with syntax. This poem, like many of the poems from the Lower Rio Grande writers circle discussed in the introduction, ironically includes Orientalist language. As with other poems, we changed Paredes' intertextual glosses from boldface to italics.

[24] Despite the irregular rhyme scheme (abba / caca / dbdb / caca / ebeb), there is some coherfence within individual stanzas. We chose to preserve as much of the rhyme scheme as possible while still giving the poem its own internal rhythm, which necessitated that we take some liberties with word choice.

[25] We chose to preserve the poem's rhyme scheme as much as possible, which required syntax, plural and word choice changes, such as using "grieve" for *llora* ("cry"), "reef" for *playas* ("shores"), "grieve" for *sinsabores*; and "bursts" for *brotar* ("emerges").

[26] This poem uses vernacular and archaic spellings (*ficiste* for *hiciste*, and *Corasón* for *Corazón*). There is an apparent typographical error in line 4, (*dolo* instead of *dolor*) but this also could be an allusion to an oral tradition, in which the "r" can be somewhat silent. (This possibility also arises from the vernacular spelling of *corazón*.) In order to approximate the rhyme scheme of the original Spanish (abba / acca / abba) we made some tactical translation decisions that slightly deviate from the original. These include changing the tense and meaning in lines 4 and 12. Thus, while the literal translation of the line is "see the pain you bring me," we chose "see the pain you devise" and "see the wrong you did devise," respectively.

[27] Because the rhyme scheme in the original was irregular (abcbb / cdcbb / ebebb) we chose instead to create a more regular internal stanza rhyme (abacc / adacc / aeacc). Here, we were more concerned with rhythm than with rhyme. The term *cirios* in line 7 is plural for *cirio*, which is a wax candle. A "zephyr" is the west wind or any gentle beeze. It also can be an article of clothing made of light material, like a shawl. On line 11 we repeated the phrase to parallel the syllables in the opening lines of the previous stanzas.

[28] We preserved the rhyme scheme of the original, which involves a rhyme between the first and fourth, and second and third lines of each stanza. This required several major changes of syntax and vocabulary. On line 3, we changed *joven* ("youth") to "lover." This is a significant change but the

carpe diem genre also allows for it. On line 4, we changed *duele* ("hurt" or "injury") to "endure." There also are several misspellings in the original. For example, on line 19, *criatura* ("beloved" or "sweet little thing") should be spelled *creatura*.

[29] The poem begins with alternating rhyming couplets that are broken in the final stanza (abab / cdcd / efef / ghggh). We preserved the rhyme within individual stanzas but changed the last stanza to preserve the translation's internal rhythm.

[30] We added "tart" to line 5 to preserve the rhyme even though this term is more of a British colloquialism. The *Rima* genre that Paredes invokes, however, allows for this intercultural term since the original poem essentially is a love poem to a "nubile" virgin (*virgen angélica*).

[31] Gustavo Adolfo Becquer was a nineteenth-century Spanish poet. Paredes' use of "Julia" is a reference to Julia Espín, who was the daughter of a prominent muscian and subsequently became the Becquer's muse. Although she cared for Becquer, she apparently never considered him a proper suitor. Becquer nonetheless dedicated most of his poetry, especially his short trite love poems, or *Rimas*, to her. We added some superlatives to the last two lines to preserve the internal rhythm of the translation.

[32] This poem is Paredes' translation of John Donne's 1616 original of the same title. Paredes translated the poem into contemporary Spanish, but since the poem essentially is the same, we have used Donne's English original instead of translating Paredes' version.

[33] The original poem uses an assonant rhyme scheme for the first stanza (abab) and a consonant rhyme scheme for the second. We chose to use consonant rhyme scheme in our translation while attempting to preserve the meter and rhythm of the overall composition. This requires dome significant deviation from the original. In the first stanza, we changed the subjunctive tense with an affirmation on line 4, which is suggested by the exclamation marks. On line 2, we used "sound" for *voz* ("voice"), and on line 5 we changed *luz de plata* ("light of silver" or "silver light") to "silver light shade."

[34] The rhyme scheme involves rhymes between the first and third, as well as the second and fourth lines in each stanzas, which we preserved. On line 5, *si de modo de* should be *si el modo de*, which we took huge liberties for the sake of preserving the tempo. Paredes also uses similar idiosyncratic spellings on line 12, in which he writes *de desear* instead of *al desear*, which we translated as "for desiring." We also changed *astro* to "star's orbit," which is consistent with the context.

Paredes' use of the Italian spelling for *Beatrice* (bee-ah-tree-che) rhymes with *desdicha*. The reference is to Dante's Beatrice, the poet's beloved for whom he traveled to Hell in order to be with her again. *Dulcinea* is Don

Quijote's love interest, or rather, his damsel and muse, in Miguel de Cervantes' sixteenth-centry picaresque, *Las aventuras de Don Quijote*. Dulcinea, who appears as a noble maiden to Don Quijote, who himself is a farmer delusioned into thinking he was a knight from the small village of La Mancha, is in actuality a barmaid in a country inn. Both these references invoke the theme of loss and the attendant pain. They also enable Paredes to create an existentialist mediation on poetry and thus the poem reads as another ars poetica.

[35] This *Rima* is indicative of the love limericks popularized by Becquer.

[36] The epigraph from this poem is apparently from a poem by Manuel Cruz, a member of the Lower Rio Grande writer's circle discussed in the introduction. The specific poem that Paredes glosses apparently is lost. The consonant rhyme scheme involves the first and third as well as the second and fourth lines in each stanza, which we sought to preserve.

[37] The first stanza in this poem is taken from a poem by Roberto Ramírez Ramírez, a childhood friend of Paredes from Brownsville and a member of the Lower Rio Grande Writer's circle. This stanza gloss also opens the first of Paredes' two poems titled *Juguete*, which we titled "Toy (I)."

[38] Our translation attempts to preserve the assonant rhyme scheme of the original, which follows an "aaba" rhyme scheme in the first two stanzas, with the third stanza written as "baba" for crescendo. However, in order to preserve the rhyme, we Anglicized *Carolina* as "Caroline," which was the referent's actual name. As noted in the introduction, Caroline was an Anglo American girl with blond hair and green eyes, and apparently the poet's first love interest. He dedicated two planned poetry collections to her, "Black Roses" and *Cantos a Carolina*, the later being excerpted in *Between Two Worlds*. According to evidence in the Américo Paredes Papers, he continued to write poems to or about her until the mid-1940s, around the time of his first marriage. As noted in the introduction, in an April 18, 1979 journal entry, Paredes later refers to her as a "daughter of the enemy."

[39] This poem follows a highly irregular yet systematic rhyme scheme (abcb / defe // eghg), which we preserved.

[40] We changed the original rhyme (from abba / cddc / effe / bggb, to abba / cddc / effe / agga), to preserve the rhythm in English. In line 3, we refered to the night as "ours" instead of *la bella* ("the beautiful" or "the precious"), which is consistent with the context. In line 6, we used "within" instead of *cuerpo* ("body") for the same reasons.

[41] We chose to translate *horas felices* as "Good Times" instead of the more literal "Happy Hours" because the former is a more coherent and common idiomatic phrase in English. We preserved the irregular rhyme scheme (abacd / dada / efef / ghgh // ijij / klkl / abacd). The first stanza serves as a

refrain that is repreated in the last stanza, and apparently is a gloss from another poem that is not identified. We translated the formal plural you, *vosotros*, form in lines 22 and 23 with a redundant use of "you."

[42] This poem has an irregular but deliberate assonant rhyme scheme (abbaab / cddccd / effefe). The first two lines of each stanza form a refrain, and the refrain in the last stanza is a fusion of the first two lines of the stanza. On line 4, we changed *abrojos* ("thistles") to "frailties," and on line 15 we extended *¡qué pureza!* ("What purity!"), to "Such a pure blush!"

[43] As with many of Paredes' *Rimas*, this poem's rhyme scheme is only partially successful. Paredes' intent obviously is to rhyme the first and third lines of each stanza but from the fourth stanza onwards, the rhyme scheme breaks down. We attempted to create internal rhythms within each stanza.

[44] Francis Jammes was a French poet and novelist (1868-1938) renowned for his pastoral themes. He was a prominent influence on many pre-WWII poets in Europe and the U.S.

[45] Paredes set this sonnet to music and composed a simple Tango beat for the guitar (see Figure 48). Paredes wrote an English version of this poem, which apparently is lost. As noted in the introduction, we translated *mujer* as "girl" instead of "woman." Paredes' age, the context of the poem, and his own attitudes and vocabulary about women expressed in archive materials, suggests that this would be his own English equivalent. We translated *payo*, which literarlly means "rustic," as *payaso*, or "clown," in order to preserve the rhyme.

[46] The English version is the original by Alfred Lord Tennyson written in 1889.

[47] In line 3 we made a figural translation of *tu mente nunca supo la niñez* (literally, "your mind never knew of or had a childhood") to "your mind never wore a childhood dress," since the line is more of an idiomatic phrase. On line 4, we translated *judicial* as "judicial" instead of the more literal "judicious" to preserve the rhyme of the Petrarchan sonnet. The poem also uses convoluted tenses, such as in the final stanza where Paredes blends past, present, and future tenses. We approximated the original but privileged the rhyme and syntax of the English.

[48] This poem is one of several anagrams Paredes wrote, some of which are embedded in personal letters. We took some liberties in the translation of certain terms in order to preserve the anagram "GABRIEL M," as well as the alternating rhyme scheme. No information about the referent was found in the archives.

[49] Paredes' sister Blanca, pictured with her brother in Figure 30 on the occasion of her First Communion, died in her childhood. Paredes dedicated several poems, including the following poem, "To Blanca."

[50] In line 8 we translated *dolor del cuello* as "pain in my brain" instead of the literal "pain in the neck," which has a different idiomatic resonance ("nuisance") that is inconsistent with the theme of loss. We used "brain" because the poet seeks to express that neither intellect, body nor artistry are enough to convey the pain of this loss.

[51] Paredes uses the formal plural "you," or *vosotros,* conjugation in this poem, which we have approximated with redundant elevated diction.

[52] The irregular rhyme scheme of this limerick is nonetheless deliberate (abbc / deec). Pursuant to preserving this rhyme, we changed *nací* ("was born") on line 4 to "ushered."

[53] In line 3 we use the Spanish *cítara* since the English word, "zithern" (or "cithern") is so uncommon. As noted in the introduction, the *cítara* is an ancient Greek stringed instrument of the lyre class similar to a guitar. We preserved the irregular rhyme scheme abcb / cdad by making necessary idiomatic changes. For instance, on line 6, we translated *bestia soñadora* ("dreaming beast") to "daydreaming beast" since this is the correct connotation.

[54] In lines 7 and 10, we translated *¡Ay, de los labios callados!* as "Oh, of those silent lips," because the previous lines suggest the personification of the emotions (*las pasiones*) and related body parts like lips. The *¡Ay!* thus is both an exasperation uttered by the poet but also by the referent, in this case lips.

[55] There apparently is a typographical error on line 12 of the original Spanish version. The term *anima* ("animate") should be the plural *animan*. On line 19, *ha varias* should be *hace* or *hay*, which would translate as "there are many." On line 20, we translated *otra faz nueva, plácida y serena*, as "a new, placid and serene grace," since the context alludes more to an aura than a literal face. On line 23, we translated *malhayan* ("they find themselves in a bad position") as "useless" as this is an idiomatic contraction with no coherent literal translation.

As a classical pianist, Paredes would have known of the classical music love song genre known as the nocturne, but he transforms the romantic theme with an existentialist one. As recounted in Note 17 above, this poem is one of Paredes' "Night" poems.

[56] Paredes apparently had a Petrarchan sonnet in mind, but since the rhyme scheme of the form is not maintained, we structured the poem around three stanzas with alternate lines rhyming (abab / cdcd / efefef).

[57] *Décimas* are Spanish stanzas consisting of ten verses of (usually) eight syllables. The form is distinguished by its dialogue with other poets. Indeed, a *décima* oftentimes includes a gloss of another poet's *décima*. The form has a variety of themes and oftentimes is put to accoustic music. This is one of the Mexican folk forms Paredes is renowned for recupering.

Paredes, like his relatives and other members of the Lower Rio Grande Writer's Circle, was an accomplished writer of *décimas*, and his archives include dozens of examples written by him and his poetic compatriots.

[58] The opening refrain follows an *abba* pattern. The complex network of rhymes in all *décimas*, which is facilitated in Romance languages like Spanish, varies widely but always involves internally rhymed stanzas, each with at least three different rhymes. This rhyme pattern is difficult to approximate in English, so in order to preserve the rhyme scheme, which is fundamental to the genre, we made selections of words and phrases that sometimes deviate widely from the original.

[59] This French term usually is translated as "envoy" or "messenger." This reference has a mulitiplicity of possible meanings, and in this context there also appears to be a neoclassical allusion as well as an existentialist allusion since the succeeding poem concerns the author's journey in life towards death.

[60] On line 4, we translated *el futuro ignoto que me espera* ("the unknown future that awaits me") as "unknown future maze" since the temporal dimension already is established in preceding lines. This enabled us to preserve the Sonnet rhyme scheme of the poem. Not only is the existentialist theme similar to the theme expressed in other poems but Paredes also glosses a preceding *Rima* in some lines of this poem.

[61] *Flor y Canto II: An Anthology of Chicano Literature.* Eds. Arnoldo C. Vento, Alurista, José Flores Peregrino. Austin: Pajarito Publications, 1975. p. 34.

[65] *Between Two Worlds*. Houston: Arte Público Press, 1991. Pp. 35-6.

Note on Translators

B.V. Olguín was born and raised in Houston, Texas. He received a BA with Honors from the University of Houston and a MA and PhD from Stanford University. He has published poetry in a variety of journals in English and presently is completing two poetry collections, *Sombras de Sangre/Shadows of Blood*, and *In This Corner: Boxing Poems in Prose*. He presently works as an Assistant Professor in the Department of English, Classics and Philosophy at the University of Texas at San Antonio. He teaches Chicana/o, Multi-Ethnic, Latin American and Postcolonial Literatures and has published research articles in journals such as *Cultural Critique*, *American Literary History* and *Aztlán*. His book, *La Pinta: History, Culture and Ideology in Chicana/o Convict Discourse* is forthcoming from the University of Texas Press in 2008.

Omar Vásquez Barbosa was born and raised in Mexico City. He received a BA from Shriner University in Kerrville, Texas and a MA in English from the University of Texas at San Antonio. He is an accomplished poet and playwright and has published several poems in Spanish and English in journals in the U.S. and Mexico. He presently is studying film in Barcelona, Spain.

Recovering the U.S. Hispanic Literary Heritage Series

Recovering the U.S. Hispanic Literary Heritage Volume V
Kenya Dworkin y Méndez and
Agnes Lugo-Ortiz, Editors
May 31, 2006, 240 pages, Clothbound
ISBN: 978-1-55885-371-3, $39.95

Hispanic Periodicals in the United States, Origins to 1960: A Brief History and Comprehensive Bibliography
Nicolás Kanellos with Helvetia Martell
2000, 368 pages, Clothbound
ISBN 1-55885-253-0, $69.95

Firefly Summer
Pura Belpré
1996, 205 Pages, Trade Paperback
ISBN 1-55885-180-1, $9.95
Accelerated Reader Quiz #35001

A Nation of Women: An Early Feminist Speaks Out / Mi opinión sobre las libertades, derechos y deberes de la mujer
Luisa Capetillo
English translation by Alan West-Durán
Introduction by Félix V. Matos Rodríguez
2004, 224 pages, Trade Paperback
ISBN 1-55885-427-4, $16.95

Cantares: Canticles and Poems of Youth
Fray Angélico Chávez
Introduction by Nasario García
2000, 134 pages, Trade Paperback
ISBN 1-55885-311-1, $12.95

Lo que el pueblo me dice
Jesús Colón
Edited, with an Introduction by Edwin Karli Padilla Aponte
2001, 272 pages, Trade Paperback
ISBN 1-55885-330-8, $12.95

The Way It Was and Other Writings
Jesús Colón; Edited by Edna Acosta-Belén and Virginia Sánchez Korrol
1993, 128 Pages, Trade Paperback
ISBN 1-55885-057-0, $12.00

Pioneros puertorriqueños en Nueva York 1917–1947
Joaquín Colón;
Preface by Olimpia Colón-Aponte
Introduction by Edwin Karli Padilla Aponte
2001, 380 pages, Trade Paperback
ISBN 1-55885-335-9, $12.95

Tropical Town and Other Poems
Salomón de la Selva
Edited, with an Introduction, by Silvio Sirias
1998, 256 pages, Trade Paperback
ISBN 1-55885-235-2, $12.95

History and Legends of the Alamo and Other Missions in and around San Antonio
Adina de Zavala; Edited by Richard Flores
1996, 215 Pages, Trade Paperback
ISBN 1-55885-181-X, $12.95

Journey to the United States of America / Viaje a los Estados Unidos del Norte de América
Lorenzo de Zavala
English translation by Wallace Woolsey
Edited and with an introduction by John-Michael Rivera
2005, 496 pages, Trade Paperback
ISBN 1-55885-453-3, $16.95

Dew on the Thorn
Jovita González; Edited by José Limón
1997, 181 Pages, Trade Paperback
ISBN 1-55885-175-5, $12.95

The Woman Who Lost Her Soul and Other Stories
Jovita González; Edited, with an Introduction, by Sergio Reyna
2000, 160 Pages, Trade Paperback
ISBN 1-55885-313-8, $12.95

Black Cuban, Black American: A Memoir
Evelio Grillo
Introduction by Kenya Dworkin-Mendez
2000, 152 pages, Trade Paperback
ISBN 1-55885-293-X, $13.95
Contains an eight page photo insert

Lucas Guevara
Alirio Díaz Guerra
English translation by Ethriam Cash Brammer
Introduction by Nicolás Kanellos and Imara Liz Hernández
Facsimile edition with illustrations
2003, 336 pages, Trade Paperback
ISBN 1-55885-390-1, $12.95

Also available in the original Spanish:
Lucas Guevara
Alirio Díaz Guerra
Facsimile edition with illustrations
2001, 256 pages, Trade Paperback
ISBN 1-55885-325-1, $12.95

Recovering the U.S. Hispanic Literary Heritage Series

Versos sencillos / Simple Verses
José Martí
English translation by Manuel A. Tellechea
1997, 128 Pages, Trade Paperback
ISBN 1-55885-204-2, $12.95

Selected Poems / Poesía selecta
Luis Palés Matos
English translation and Introduction by
Julio Marzán
2000, 224 pages, Trade Paperback
ISBN 1-55885-303-0, $12.95

The Collected Stories of María Cristina Mena
María Cristina Mena
Edited by Amy Doherty
1997, 208 Pages, Trade Paperback
ISBN 1-55885-211-5, $12.95

El Laúd del Desterrado
Edited by Matías Montes-Huidobro
1995, 182 Pages, Trade Paperback
ISBN 1-55885-082-1, $10.95

The Account: Álvar Núñez Cabeza de Vaca's Relación
Edited and translated by José Fernández
and Martin Favata
1993, 156 Pages, Trade Paperback
ISBN 1-55885-060-0, $12.95

The Real Billy the Kid
Miguel Antonio Otero, Jr.
Introduction by John-Michael Rivera
1998, 224 pages, Trade Paperback
ISBN 1-55885-234-4, $12.95

Life and Adventures of the Celebrated Bandit Joaquín Murrieta
Ireneo Paz
English translation by Frances P. Belle
Introduction by Luis Leal
1999, 256 pages, Trade Paperback
ISBN 1-55885-277-8, $12.95

El Coyote, the Rebel
Luis Perez; with an Introduction by
Lauro Flores
2000, 164 pages, Trade Paperback
ISBN 1-55885-296-4, $12.95

Women's Tales from the New Mexico WPA: La Diabla a Pie
Edited by Tey Diana Rebolledo and
María Teresa Márquez
Introduction by Tey Diana Rebolledo
2000, 512 Pages, Trade Paperback
ISBN 1-55885-312-X, $17.95

Conflicts of Interest: The Letters of María Amparo Ruiz de Burton
María Amparo Ruiz de Burton
Edited, with an Introduction,
by Rosaura Sánchez and Beatrice Pita
2001, 672 pages, Trade Paperback
ISBN 1-55885-328-6, $17.95

The Squatter and the Don
María Amparo Ruiz de Burton
Edited by Rosaura Sánchez and Beatrice Pita
1997 (Second Edition), 381 Pages
Trade Paperback, ISBN 1-55885-185-2, $16.95

Who Would Have Thought It?
María Amparo Ruiz de Burton
Edited by Rosaura Sánchez and Beatrice Pita
1995, 298 Pages, Trade Paperback
ISBN 1-55885-081-3, $12.95

Jicoténcal
Félix Varela
Edited by Luis Leal and Rodolfo J. Cortina
1995, 164 Pages, Trade Paperback
ISBN 1-55885-132-1, $10.95

The Adventures of Don Chipote, or, When Parrots Breast-Feed
Daniel Venegas
English translation by Ethriam Cash Brammer
Edited, with an Introduction, by Nicolás Kanellos
2000, 168 pages, Trade Paperback
ISBN 1-55885-297-2, $12.95

Las aventuras de Don Chipote, o, Cuando los pericos mamen
Daniel Venegas; Edited, with an Introduction
by Nicolás Kanellos
1998, 208 pages, Trade Paperback
ISBN 1-55885-252-2, $12.95

The Rebel
Leonor Villegas de Magnón
Edited by Clara Lomas
1994, 297 Pages, Trade Paperback
ISBN 1-55885-056-2, $12.00